THE
RIDGEWAY

THE RIDGEWAY

Neil Curtis

Photographs by Martin Trelawney
General editor Michael Allaby

AURUM PRESS

COUNTRYSIDE COMMISSION · ORDNANCE SURVEY

ACKNOWLEDGEMENTS

In no particular order, my thanks go to the series editor, Michael Allaby, for asking me to compile this guide; to Wendy Pettigrew of the Countryside Commission for her courteous co-operation; to David Venner, the Ridgeway Officer without whose help much of the information contained here could not have been pieced together; to Martin Trelawney for providing such splendid photographs with little help from me; to Ridgeway Warden Frank Hart, for sharing his knowledge of the sheep fairs at East Ilsley; to Ken Watts for his information on Snap; to my secretary, Trisha Walters, who despite the continued machine-gun noise of the wind on my dictating machine managed to type up my notes from which I then wrote this little book; and lastly, but by no means least, to my wife Sheila Dallas, who walked with me for the first 15 miles and who then provided logistical and moral support at various intervals along the way, as well as afterwards when I was struggling to put fingers to keyboard.

Neil Curtis has a degree in geology and has worked in natural history publishing since 1971. He lives in Oxfordshire and runs his own publishing service.

This revised edition first published 1997, updated 1999, by Aurum Press Ltd in association with the Countryside Commission and the Ordnance Survey
Text copyright © 1989, 1994, 1997, 1999 by Aurum Press Ltd, the Countryside Commission and the Ordnance Survey
Maps Crown copyright © 1989, 1994, 1997, 1999 by the Ordnance Survey
Photographs copyright © 1989, 1994, 1997 by the Countryside Commission
Photographs pages 46, 110 and 115 by Jos Joslin

Ordnance Survey and Pathfinder are registered trade marks and the OS Symbol and Explorer are trade marks of Ordnance Survey, the National Mapping Agency of Great Britain.

British Library Cataloguing in Publication Data

Curtis, Neil.
The Ridgeway. – 2Rev.ed (National trail guides; 4)
Southern England. Long-distance footpaths: Ridgeway Path. Recreations: Walking – Visitors' guides
I. Title II. Series
796.5′1′09422

ISBN 1 85410 490 X
2 4 6 8 10 9 7 5 3
2000   2001   1999

Book design by Robert Updegraff
Cover photograph: Agricultural landscape at The Hale, near Wendover.
Title page photograph: the Chiltern escarpment from Watlington Hill

Typeset by Wyvern 21 Ltd, Bristol
Printed and bound in Italy by Printer Trento Srl

CONTENTS

Circular walks appear on pages 32, 52, 58, 72, 78 and 120

How to use this guide

This guide to the 85-mile (137-kilometre) national trail along the Ridgeway is in three parts:

• The introduction, with an historical background to the area and advice for walkers and riders.

• The Ridgeway itself, split into twelve chapters, with maps opposite the description for each route section. In some cases the chapters cover relatively short sections of the Ridgeway, which will make it easier for people planning day or weekend walks or rides along this national trail. The distances noted with each chapter represent the total length of the Ridgeway, including sections through towns and villages. This part of the guide also includes information on places of interest as well as a number of short walks which can be taken around the Ridgeway. There are also many other circular routes linking with the Ridgeway, details of which are included in the relevant chapters. Key sites are numbered both in the text and on the maps to make it easier to follow the route description.

• The last part includes useful information such as local transport, accommodation and organisations involved with the Ridgeway.

The maps have been prepared by Ordnance Survey® for this trail guide using 1:25000 Pathfinder®, or Explorer™ maps as a base. The line of the Ridgeway is shown in yellow, with the status of each section of the trail – footpath, bridleway or byway, for example – shown in green underneath (see key on inside front cover). These rights of way markings also indicate the precise alignment of the Ridgeway. In some cases, the yellow line on these maps may show a route which is different from that shown on older maps; you are recommended to follow the yellow route in this guide, which will be the route that is waymarked with the distinctive acorn symbol 🟤 used for all national trails. Any parts of the Ridgeway that may be difficult to follow on the ground are clearly highlighted in the route description. *Black arrows (➡) at the edge of the maps indicate the start point.*

Should there be a need to divert the Ridgeway from the route shown in this guide, for maintenance work or because the route has had to be changed, you are advised to follow any waymarks or signs along the path.

KEY MAPS INDEX

KEY MAP 1

KEY MAP 2

KEY MAP 1

KEY MAPS

The Ridgeway

Chapter start point

0 Kms   5

0 Miles   5

KEY MAP 2

Distance checklist

The following distances along the Ridgeway are included to help you plan your journey.

location	approx. distance from previous location	
	miles	*km*
Overton Hill	0	0
Barbury Castle (car park)	6.5	10.5
Ogbourne St George	2.6	4.2
Fox Hill	7.4	11.9
Ashbury (B 4000)	3.3	5.3
Uffington Castle/Whitehorse Hill	2.1	3.4
Sparsholt Firs	2.9	4.7
Manor Road (for Wantage)	3.4	5.5
Bury Down	5.7	9.2
Compton – bridleway access	2.9	4.7
Streatley (A 329)	5.2	8.4
Goring on Thames	0.4	0.6
South Stoke	1.8	2.9
North Stoke	2.3	3.7
Mongewell Park (for Wallingford)	1.2	1.9
Nuffield Common	4.0	6.4
Watlington (Hill Road)	5.4	8.7
Lewknor – road access	2.3	3.7
Chinnor	3.3	5.3
Princes Risborough (Brimmers Road)	5.3	8.5
Wendover	5.9	9.5
Wigginton	6.1	9.8
Tring Station	2.0	3.2
Ivinghoe Beacon	3.5	5.6

PREFACE

The Ridgeway National Trail, which is 85 miles long, passes through five counties in central-southern England. It follows in part an ancient green road and crosses some of our finest chalk downland landscapes.

The Ridgeway is easy to follow and the whole of the western half (43 miles, 69 km) can be enjoyed by horseriders and cyclists as well as walkers. The entire route can be comfortably walked in a week, but for the day visitor there are many shorter, circular walks utilizing sections of the route.

National Trails are promoted and funded by the Countryside Commission and maintained by local authorities. They are all waymarked with the distinctive acorn symbol, which signals that you are on the right route.

I hope that you will enjoy this book in the planning of your visit and that it will add to your pleasure on the Ridgeway.

Richard Simmonds
Chairman
Countryside Commission

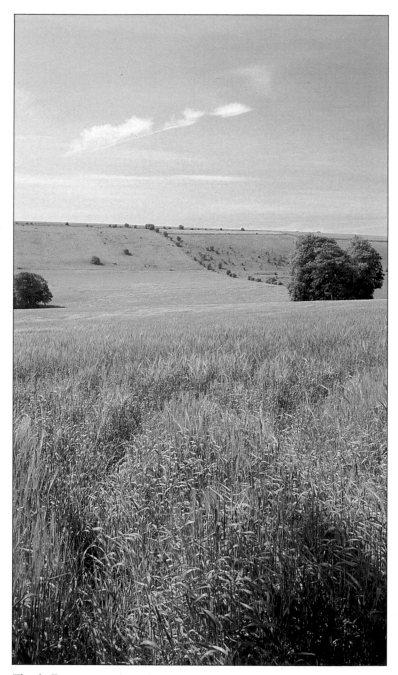

Thurle Down, near Streatley. Once the downs were predominantly grassland, but many have now been ploughed for arable crops.

PART ONE

Introduction

In *The Oldest Road: An Exploration of the Ridgeway*, J. R. L. Anderson states that 'Most roads have a beginning and an end, but the Ridgeway has neither: what is left of it, and it is a remarkable stretch for a road of such antiquity, starts nowhere and concludes in time rather than in space.' Historically and philosophically, this may be true but, for the purposes of this book and the Countryside Commission, the National Trail begins in the west at Overton Hill, beside the A4 trunk road a short distance from the village of Avebury, a World Heritage site, with its extraordinary stone circles, and stretches eastwards for some 85 miles (137 km) ending at the triangulation pillar on Ivinghoe Beacon in Buckinghamshire, to the north-east of Tring. Thus, it is a convenient and satisfying route, starting and finishing as it does on hills, with parking, bus routes, and, in the case of Tring and several other places, railway stations nearby.

Passing through five counties (Wiltshire, Oxfordshire, Berkshire, Buckinghamshire and Hertfordshire) and crossing the chalk downland of the North Wessex Downs Area of Outstanding Natural Beauty (AONB), the Ridgeway goes through the Goring Gap, before following the River Thames for a short way and rising on to the undulating hills of the Chilterns AONB via Grim's Ditch. Thus the west–east walker gradually gathers an intimate experience of the landscape of this stretch of south-central England. For those who believe that the whole of this part of the country is nothing but motorways, industrial estates and urban conurbations, to walk the Ridgeway in its entirety is an education as well as a joy. That is not to say that, from time to time, the drone of speeding motor traffic does not intrude, nor that 'civilisation' is never encountered but, for much of the way, even in the mechanised, urbanised, computerised 20th century, it is possible to feel, if not 'far from the madding crowd', at least spiritually removed and moderately distanced from it. Indeed, one of the minor problems encountered by walkers tackling the whole route is that, especially along the western 'half', to find accommodation it is necessary to leave the ridge and descend as much as 3 miles (5 km) to a village, only to have to climb up again the next day.

We might like to believe that to walk the Ridgeway from Overton Hill to Streatley before crossing the Thames is to travel along an ancient trading route, remote from our world and unspoiled by human interference. Certainly the green road is an old one and, apart from the ever-spreading sprawl of Swindon (Swine Down), there are few towns or cities to bar the way. But, in some ways, it is along the less historically authentic part of the walk, from Goring to Ivinghoe, that more traditional kinds of landscape are encountered, even though the walker passes close to, or through, a number of small towns.

It is remarkable how quickly the mind adjusts, how scenery which had scarcely changed for decades, or even centuries, can be wiped away almost overnight, and yet how soon one forgets the former and accepts the latter as 'natural' rural England. Much of the western part of the Ridgeway follows a line of chalk downland where traces of ancient field systems show that prehistoric practice was markedly different in its use of land from our own and where the blackthorn-hedged, sheep- and rabbit-cropped fields still extant in this century have given way to vast, prairie-like expanses of monoculture grazing and monotonous hybrid cereal crops. In late summer, hectare upon hectare of uniformly golden, poker-straight, tall stems wave their abundance in the wind; on the grasslands even the sheep grow more quickly, more uniformly, and with leaner meat or less oily wool to satisfy the demands of today's consumers. But still, for those young enough to know nothing different or for walkers who are new to this trail, the Ridgeway seems to fulfil a basic need in many of us: a need to get away from city hurly-burly, to breathe fresh air, to view open, rolling land, to chance upon wild plants and animals, to encounter other occasional adventurers along the way, and to spend a few days at one's own pace.

Throughout its length, the Ridgeway is a versatile route. For anyone who is physically fit and who derives pleasure from testing their body and mental fortitude against distance, it is perfectly possible to complete the whole route in four days or even less, averaging more than 20 miles (32 km) a day. Unless walking the path is an exercise in stamina, to complete it at a more leisurely and enjoyable pace should take about six days, so that a day's walk is about 12–15 miles (20–25 km). A reasonable pace to maintain is about $2\frac{1}{2}$ miles (4 km) an hour, so 15 miles (25 km) might take a little over six hours. During three seasons of the year, this leaves you with plenty of time to stand and stare, to stop for feeding and watering, to chat with companion or passerby, and to investigate an ancient hill fort or a medieval church. Even in the winter, a day's walk of this distance should be perfectly possible if you are so inclined.

But there are other ways of travelling the Ridgeway. There are circular routes for walkers or riders, both official and unofficial, based on parts of its length and up to 8 miles (12 km) or so long. There are short strolls from a car park to a hill fort or a burial chamber such as Wayland's Smithy. You could tackle, as I have done more than once, Overton Hill to Streatley and Goring to Ivinghoe as two separate long weekend walks, or either could be shortened slightly to fit comfortably into a normal weekend.

Nor are you confined to Shanks's pony, for most of the western 'half' of the path is byway or 'road used as public path' (RUPP) and parts of the eastern section are bridleway or RUPP. Horseriders and cyclists are permitted on bridleways (waymarked with blue arrows) and on byways (marked with red arrows) or RUPPs. In addition, motorcycles and other motor vehicles are permitted on byways and most RUPPs. RUPPs are an old classification and all RUPPs are being reclassified as either byways or bridleways, but this work will take some time.

To some people, motorcycles and four-wheel-drive vehicles are sometimes rather too much in evidence on the western section of the Ridgeway. In 1995 a Code of Respect was launched to attempt to reduce any potential conflicts between different users. The Code gives a clear message of the rights, responsibilities and essential courtesies expected and aims to increase awareness and respect both of other users and the Ridgeway itself. Finally, both children and adults, launching model gliders, powered craft, or even themselves attached to hang gliders, seem to find parts of the Ridgeway particularly suitable, as every walker discovers at the weekend or bank holiday in clement weather.

However you tackle the Ridgeway, it is there to be enjoyed and there is much to enjoy. From ridgetop to valley, from hill fort to chalk quarry, from trunk road to narrow track, a traveller on the Ridgeway will be accompanied by the rush of the wind, the songs of birds, the quiet rustle of wheat, and by the knowledge that he or she is following a path that has been trodden more or less continuously over much of its length for thousands of years.

History of the Ridgeway

The Ridgeway, of which the national trail forms a part, has been said to be one of the oldest 'roads' in Europe, although it seems that there is no direct evidence of its use before the Bronze Age. From the coast, perhaps near Lyme Regis in Dorset, the way stretched for more than 250 miles (400 km) in a north-easterly direction, probably reaching what is now the Wash somewhere near Hunstanton in north Norfolk. It is possible to walk this entire route today by first taking the Wessex Ridgeway (a Ramblers' Association-devised route) from Lyme Regis to Marlborough, and then the Ridgeway, and on to the Icknield Way to link with the Peddars Way, ending at Holme next the Sea.

The name 'Ridgeway' is taken from the Anglo-Saxon word 'hrycweg' and, in the various charters of their period, a complicated network of these green roads is mentioned – each usually following a natural route on high ground, thereby allowing the traveller to avoid the hazards of the densely wooded and often marshy ground of the valleys below, especially during the harsh weather of winter.

Most authorities agree, however, that the western half of the Ridgeway, in particular, must have been used as a drove road, a trading route, and as a convenient means for invaders, peaceful or war-like, to penetrate the heartland of southern England long before Anglo-Saxon or even Roman times, not least because of the numbers and scale of hill forts and ancient and important religious centres that grew up along its way, the remains of which we can still see today.

It is tempting to suppose that one is walking on identical ground to that trodden by the ancients. However, until about 200 years ago, the Ridgeway was a broad band of tracks along the crest of the Downs, or, in the case of the Icknield Way, beneath the scarp of the Chilterns. People walked, rode their horses or drove their sheep and cattle along the driest or most convenient track.

It was the Enclosure Acts of 1750–1800 that defined, for each parish, the course and exact width of the Ridgeway. For most parishes this was set at 40 feet (12 metres), for others at as much as 66 feet (20 metres). The banks and thorn hedges alongside the Ridgeway date from this period and were put there to prevent livestock from straying into the newly cultivated arable fields.

It is largely in this century that the present system of main, trunk and motorway roads has come into being, with some following the lines of older routes, such as Roman roads. And with the coming of the new means of communication, so the old ways have fallen into disuse except as convenient access roads for farmers or as footpaths and rights of way for today's nomads – walkers, horseriders and cyclists. Thus, in most places, only fragments of these ancient ways survive and we are fortunate that so much of the Ridgeway is now preserved.

The idea for a long-distance route following the line of the Chilterns and the Wessex chalk downs was first mooted in 1947 in a report by the Hobhouse Committee. The present route was approved by the Secretary of State for the Environment in 1972 and so began yet another phase in the long history of an ancient green road. Today, there is a small team of staff based with Oxfordshire County Council's Department of Leisure and Arts, whose task it is to manage the National Trail.

Practical advice

Walking, cycling or riding a horse on the Ridgeway does not require the same precautions as pursuing these activities on a mountain in Wales or Scotland. The weather is rarely very severe; it is hard to get lost; the going underfoot is not dangerous and is, at worst, wet and rutted; and you are seldom far from help should it be needed. On the other hand, there is no point in making life difficult for yourself and a few simple precautions should enhance your enjoyment.

If you are walking, the single most important piece of equipment to get right is footwear. Almost everyone who ever sets foot to footpath has a different view on what it is best to wear on the feet but one thing is certain, unless you usually live in them, you don't need foot-dragging heavy mountain boots here. For short walks, especially during winter or spring when parts of the way might be very boggy, wellington boots or one of the other kinds of rubber boots now available are as good as anything. But I would not advise wearing wellies for more than a day. For me the best compromise is a pair of modern lightweight walking boots or shoes.

Clothing, too, has come a long way since the mandatory tweeds and cords for the great outdoors but again it's up to you to find out what suits you best. For three seasons of the year, a pair of polycotton walking trousers, a shirt, a spare sweater or thermofleece garment, and a waterproof (preferably breathable)

Ogbourne St George, the only village to be found on the western section of the Ridgeway.

are all you really need. In winter, extra warm clothing, a hat and gloves are a good idea.

If I am out for the day or longer, I usually carry a small first-aid kit containing some aspirin, plasters, some 'moleskin', 'animal wool', or chiropodist's felt, a tube of antiseptic cream and, during the season, some antihistamine cream.

Especially on the western half of the walk, where pubs and cafés are well off the path, you will need to take some spare food and drink with you on a longer trip. For me it's usually a flask of coffee, an aluminium bottle of fresh water, a hunk of cheese, some wholemeal bread or rolls, something sweet, and something fruity. On the other hand, some people prefer to content themselves with a hearty breakfast and walk through until the end of the day and a substantial dinner.

This guide book, together with the signs and waymarks you will find along the whole length of the path, will enable you easily to follow the route without any other assistance although, from time to time, signs do get vandalised. You do not necessarily require one, but it can be very satisfying to carry a compass with you and know how to use it. If nothing else, it might enable you more easily to identify features off the track.

To carry your bits and pieces, you will need a rucksack. Buy the best that you can afford. Try several sorts for comfort (especially with some weight in it) and access to its various pockets and compartments. It's very frustrating to have to undo lots of buckles, strings and zips and then empty the whole thing just to find your sandwiches at lunchtime. Remember, though, that even if you treat the seams with a sealing compound, rucksacks are rarely completely waterproof and it's a good idea to contain most of your belongings inside plastic bags within the rucksack. Don't be tempted to load up with the kitchen sink – a loaded rucksack will become very heavy after the first mile or two. Keep the weight down! Also, do remember that you should not leave any valuables in your car – take all cameras, money, etc. with you.

It is possible to find places to camp at intervals along most of the route although, unless you are on an official camp site where you will need to check in anyway, you must always seek permission to do so. There is a very wide variety of 'hi-tech' and 'not-so-hi-tech' lightweight tents to choose from. But, if you camp, you will need a bigger rucksack to cope with your tent and sleeping bag. Of course, it is perfectly possible to walk the whole route making use of youth hostels, guest houses, inns and hotels. Details of accommodation can be found on pp. 137–8.

Extensive repairs have been carried out to the path in many places but there are still areas where horseriders and cyclists might find the going heavy after wet weather. In a dry summer ruts can set rock hard and flints might occasionally puncture feet or tyres. But if these difficulties are avoided, the whole of the western half, and the Icknield Way section from west of Watlington to east of Chinnor, will provide pleasant and challenging conditions for two to three days' riding. If you wish to link these two sections, there is the Swan's Way Long Distance Bridleway, set up by Buckinghamshire County Council, which runs from Goring on Thames via the Icknield Way to Chinnor and then northwards to Salcey Forest in Northamptonshire; and from Chinnor the Icknield Way Riders' Route takes you almost to the end of the Ridgeway, at Pitstone Hill, just 1¼ miles (2 km) from Ivinghoe Beacon. Details of accommodation on the Ridgeway sections – for both horse and rider – will be found on pages 137–9.

PART TWO

THE RIDGEWAY

The 'grey wethers' – sarsen stones – on Overton Down. The boulders consist of cemented sandstone.

1 Overton Hill to Ogbourne St George

via Barbury Castle and Smeathe's Ridge
9 miles (14.7 km)

We begin our journey at the junction of the western end of the Ridgeway with the A4 trunk road at Overton Hill **1**, some 4½ miles (7 km) west of the attractive Wiltshire town of Marlborough with its many shops, pubs and cafés. No visit to this part of England or any Ridgeway expedition would be complete, however, without exploring the village of Avebury **2** with its extraordinary stone circles and other features of interest (see page 34). Avebury is about 1½ miles (2.5 km) to the north-west of our starting point and can be reached by driving for a little under three-quarters of a mile (1 km) along the A4 Devizes road and then turning right almost opposite West Kennett Farm on to the B4003, which takes you into the partially restored and so-called Stone Avenue leading to the Avebury monument.

Although it requires some forward planning, it is perfectly possible to reach Overton Hill by public transport. To help you plan, a free Public Transport Guide is published annually by the National Trails Office (see page 141), which is intended to make the Ridgeway more accessible for those without their own transport and to encourage others to leave their cars at home. If your intention is to walk the whole of the Ridgeway and you do not wish to use public transport, then perhaps you can persuade someone to take you there; if you are planning merely a day's or half day's walk and you are walking with a companion, then you can leave a car at each end of the section where there is suitable parking space. Even though there is adequate parking at Overton Hill, actually getting in and out of the parking area can be hazardous because of the busy A4 road at this point. When approaching from either direction, turning off the road must be undertaken near the brow of the hill and the view of the road from either side is limited, so it is vital to signal well in advance and to leave or rejoin the road as quickly as is safely possible.

If you are planning to leave your car for any length of time, however, there is hard standing for quite a few cars on the entrance to the path itself.

If you do use public transport, you can reach Overton Hill by using the rail service to Swindon or Pewsey (see page 34 for route from Pewsey to Overton Hill) and/or buses from Swindon, Devizes and Marlborough to Avebury or West and East Kennett. From Avebury, it is then just a short road walk to the start of the route, or the Ridgeway can be picked up a little further along its way by following Green Street or the Herepath **3** (a name derived from the Old English word 'here', meaning army, and indicating that the path was wide enough for an army to use it), which runs roughly north-east out of Avebury rings. This option avoids having to walk along any busy roads and can, therefore, be more pleasant than starting from Overton Hill. Also, if you are walking east to west, it provides a marvellous descent directly to Avebury, where the tea rooms (open only in the summer) and the pub will be most welcome.

At Overton Hill **1** the Ridgeway is clearly indicated by a signpost. Ancient history soon makes its presence felt again; a small collection of round barrows can be seen to the right of the beginning of the route. From Overton Hill, head almost due north and on to the Marlborough Downs – here known as Overton Down with Fyfield Down to the east.

As the route takes you uphill – steadily at first and then in more up-and-down fashion – the downlands to right and left are open and undulating. The fields are large, bounded mainly by fences and barbed or pig wire, and there are few trees. After a little over a mile (about 2 km) of comparatively easy walking along a wide track, two groups of round barrows, capped with beech trees planted to Victorian times, come into view. Presumably, the trees remain because the mounds resist the plough although, despite evidence of some arable planting, this is mainly sheep- and cattle-grazing land. To the east of the track, the Ordnance Survey map suggests that there is evidence of Iron Age field systems and, although to the untrained eye they may not be obvious, some very low, quite straight banks bounding square or rectangular areas can be seen (or imagined?).

About 1½ miles (a little over 2 km) from Overton Hill, the Ridgeway route comes to a crossing of ways on Overton Down. To the south, from whence you have come, are Overton Hill and the Bath Road, and ahead, in a direction a little east of north, are Hackpen Hill and Barbury Castle. To the west is Avebury, via the Herepath mentioned earlier, and to the east is Fyfield Down National Nature Reserve **4**. This has been described as one of the best preserved areas of ancient landscape in the vicinity. Throughout the 1960s, excavations carried out here by the

Contours are given in metres
The vertical interval is 5m

East Kennett
Long Barrow

archaeologist Peter Fowler revealed evidence of agriculture, burial sites, settlements and of other features which might unravel the mysteries of what may have been a considerable civilisation.

Shortly after the crossing of these ancient tracks, you pass another footpath off to the right and aiming in a south-easterly direction. Hereabouts, to the left of the path, there is evidence of earthworks on the hill, while on the right the 'Pits (dis)', as shown on the Ordnance Survey map, are quite clearly visible. However, of the sarsen stones – the 'Grey Wethers', as they are sometimes called – I could see little from the Ridgeway, although they are to be found on Monkton Down and Fyfield Down (see page 39).

This length of Ridgeway between Fyfield and Monkton Down reveals some interesting contrasts in flora, as well as being one of the quieter stretches where bird song and the wind in the trees are the only sounds you will hear. From the chalky soils of Fyfield Down, supporting short downland grasses, vetches and orchids, the soil becomes slightly acid as a result of clay overlying the chalk. Here, profuse hedgerows close in, long grasses and nettles predominate on the verges, and the occasional gorse bush is seen.

A little beyond Monkton Down there are more disused pits on the left, and here the track takes a sharp right and left before continuing more or less northwards again. At this point there is a junction with another path, again to the south-east, which leads to Rockley and passes through Totterdown Wood. (Note: some of the rights of way shown on the map to the west of the Ridgeway here have altered). The track climbs a little more, reaching a height of some 900 feet (270 metres) here, and continues its undulating way on high ground passing Berwick Bassett Down on the left, finally ascending again almost to the summit of Hackpen Hill with its trig point a little to the right of the Ridgeway.

A little before Hackpen Hill, the route turns slightly, taking on a north-easterly direction and then, once the hill has been passed, reaches the minor road between the village of Broad Hinton to the north-west and Marlborough to the south-east. There is room here to park a few cars and there is a good panoramic view across the plain where the villages of Broad Hinton and Winterbourne Bassett are clearly visible. Also from here, to the south-west, can be seen the smallish, roughly circular knob of Windmill Hill 5, lying the other side of Winterbourne

Monkton. Windmill Hill is the site of another Neolithic monument, known as a causewayed enclosure, built about 3400 BC. It has been suggested that this 'camp' was a sort of New Stone Age social centre, and probably continued in use for almost 1,500 years.

From the road, the still-broad track after a few hundred metres descends a little but then again reaches a height of over 900 feet (270 metres) after another half mile (1 km) or so of walking. To the right is Preshute Down.

From here, the way begins to descend, bears a little more easterly, and then the impressive ramparts of Barbury Castle **6**

Contours are given in metres
The vertical interval is 5m

rear up ahead and to the right. As you reach the foot of Barbury Castle you meet a partially metalled road leading eventually to Wroughton in the north. Here the ancient Ridgeway, as marked on the Ordnance Survey map and according to other sources, branches left and heads north-east to the left of the lower slopes of the castle towards Chiseldon, which is some 4 miles (6 km) away.

The Ridgeway National Trail, however, avoids the uninspiring village of Chiseldon, as well as some rather boring road walking, by taking you up the steep slopes to the top of the castle, across its interior, and then heads past the information centre and along the right edge of the car park before heading towards Smeathe's Ridge.

The name Barbury is probably derived from the Anglo-Saxon 'Beran Byrg', which means 'Bera's Hill' after the Saxon chief, Bera, whose victory in AD 565 over the indigenous Romano-British forces effectively brought the latter's resistance to invasion to an end. This victory heralded the real beginning of the Anglo-Saxon period even though Saxon mercenaries had been brought to Britain by the Romans as early as the turn of the 5th century, and Saxon forces had been pushing steadily westwards from about AD 440 until AD 500.

Contours are given in metres
The vertical interval is 5m

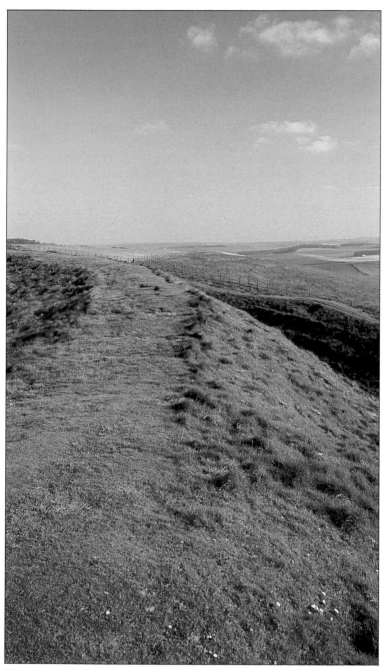

The ramparts of Barbury Castle, a hill fort used from Iron Age to Saxon times.

Today, the lush turf and imposing ramparts of Barbury Castle provide an ideal spot to sit and muse on these historical events and, in fact, the area was established as a country park in 1972. To the east of the hill fort is a car park with a stone-built plinth carrying a steel plaque erected jointly by the Automobile Association and Wiltshire County Council to commemorate the official opening of the park. There is ample parking here **7**, toilets, information panels and refreshments at the warden's bungalow. (See page 56 for information about hill forts.) From the car park, you emerge along the path to reach the narrow, metalled road which approaches the car park entrance from the north. Turn right and it quickly deteriorates into a rough track, once again running south-eastwards, and passing the buildings of Upper Herdswick Farm on the left. Shortly after you have passed the farm, take the signposted turning off the track to the left on to the broad path running through grassland on either side, which takes you on to Smeathe's Ridge **8**.

Smeathe's Ridge is a prominent north-west to south-east feature in the landscape here, continuing for at least 1½ miles (2.5 km) towards Coombe Down to the west of Ogbourne St George. This is another ancient route, thought to have been used when the lower 'Old Ridgeway' across the plain was too wet. On either side of the chalk ridge the rounded hill slopes away quite sharply from its maximum elevation of over 700 feet (220 metres) so that the views to north and south are panoramic and there is a sense of space and airiness as you wander along the broad, grassy, gently undulating track. The scenery all around is now open, rolling farmland, with few fences or hedges. To right and left there is the occasional clump of trees and views of a delightfully located racecourse to the south.

As I walked along one early spring morning, I was accompanied by the irregular shot-gun reports of automatic bird scarers which punctuated the more pleasing refrain of skylarks spiralling upwards in their songflight. After crossing a cattle grid the route follows a post and wire fence before bearing left to another catttle grid. The track continues to bear to the south-east with the high ground of Ogbourne Down and Coombe Down to the south and south-east respectively. There is some scattered evidence of the existence of tumuli here. After the cattle grid take the track which carries straight on and not the one heading uphill to the right. The path descends somewhat and at this point look for the signs of erosion and soil creep on the hill to the right. After a gate the track passes a reservoir with an ugly

Contours are given in metres
The vertical interval is 5m

concrete building between two grassy mounds. Continue down towards the narrow north–south road which takes a slightly offbeat route between Chiseldon to the north and Ogbourne St George. As you gradually lose height you reach another gate, at which point the path becomes a more obvious farm track between scrubby hedges.

Arriving at the road, turn right – the direction at this point is quite clearly indicated by the Ridgeway signpost. After about 100 yards (90 metres) the road turns sharply left and leads into the village of Ogbourne St George **9** itself. You can choose to detour through the village for refreshment or accommodation, or carry on along the Ridgeway which is signposted on the track to the right.

As you walk down the road to the village the red-brick, Georgian-style manor house comes into view on the left and close by is a grey, stone-built church. On the right is the attractive Tudor-style cottage known as The Kemms. As you approach the pubs and the main A345 road, the quaint village gives way to less appealing buildings and fast cars. There is a frequent, weekday Swindon to Marlborough bus service.

A CIRCULAR WALK FROM BARBURY CASTLE

7¾ miles (12.5 km) (see maps on pages 28–33)

From Barbury Castle **6** and the car park **7**, follow the Ridgeway route eastwards, as described in the main text, along Smeathe's Ridge to the road just before Ogbourne St George **9**. Again turn right and follow the Ridgeway route but, after about half a mile (1 km), instead of turning left to Southend, continue straight on a little to the west of south to Ogbourne St Andrew. Follow the footpath past the church and on to Ogbourne Maizey where the path joins the road. Turn right and continue more or less westwards on the right of way which leaves the hamlet. The way turns to the north-west and then north, with gallops to the right for much of the way. (If the gallops are in use, short diversions may be indicated.) Continue back to Barbury Castle, along what was once an old coaching route between Swindon and Marlborough.

A leaflet giving further details of this walk is included in the *Ridgeway Routes Pack*, along with details of other circular walks and rides, available from the National Trails Office (see page 141).

An alternative beginning: Pewsey to Overton Hill

An optional start (or end) to your Ridgeway journey is from Pewsey station, some 6 miles (10 km) from Overton Hill. It is a splendid excursion with some attractive scenery *en route*.

As you come out of Pewsey station, turn left and walk along the road to Pewsey Wharf, where there is a car park and toilets. Then take the Kennet and Avon Canal towpath in a westerly direction until you reach the second road bridge, at Wilcot. Turn right on to the minor road towards Alton Priors. About 200 yards after the second turning to the right, signposted to Stowell and Oare, the road makes a sharp, left-hand bend. At this point, take the green lane on the right (Workway Drove). Continue uphill past Pewsey Downs National Nature Reserve until you reach the road. Cross into the field opposite and then bear right and follow the fence which leads uphill to Wansdyke. From Wansdyke, carry straight on along a track, muddy in wet weather, through the woodland. Ignore any paths on left or right. Continue on, descending gradually towards East Kennett. At the road turn left into the village and then right, signposted to West Overton. After about 100 yards carry straight on into a lane, keeping the stone wall on your left. Cross a bridge and walk up the left edge of the field to the Sanctuary, then cross the A4 with care to Overton Hill.

The Avebury area

It is not uncommon that prehistoric, or even more recent historical, remains are less awe-inspiring on the ground than they appear on the map or from scientific descriptions proclaiming their archaeological significance. A good example of this is the so-called Sanctuary **10**, where all you can see is a pattern of concrete posts marking the points where stones and posts are said once to have stood. For all the casual observer can believe, the posts may be some kind of scientific practical joke! Not so with Silbury Hill, West Kennett Long Barrow **12**, Stonehenge, or especially the Avebury Stone Circles **2**. Indeed, in the latter case, the extraordinary nature of the megalithic construction almost beggars description. In the 18th century, though, even this prehistoric temple was not respected by local builders of a different age. They discovered that the stone from which the monument was constructed was good for more modern building work, and thus the temple, which had taken so much human effort to erect, was reduced to shattered remains.

Contours are given in metres
The vertical interval is 10m

Scale is approx 1¼ inches to 1 mile

35

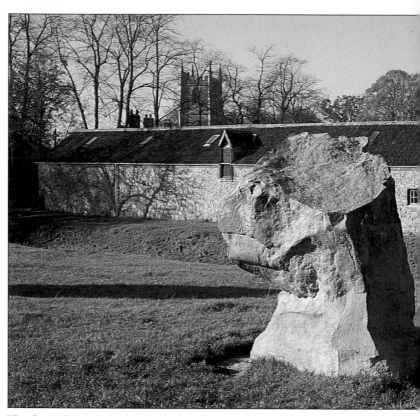

The Great Barn at Avebury housing the Wiltshire Folk Life Museum.

Avebury

A visit to the Alexander Keiller Museum at Avebury, opened in 1938 and refurbished in 1989, will, through its displays, reveal a great deal about the cultures which held this spot in such high religious regard. Alexander was a Keiller of marmalade fame, and he lived in Avebury Manor from 1936 until he died in 1955. The land he acquired, and on which he began his excavations in 1934, was obtained by the National Trust in 1942 through a public appeal for funds. Avebury Stone Circle **2** is the largest monument of its kind in Britain, and possibly in the world. It dates from the late Neolithic period and was, therefore, constructed some 4,000 years ago. It consists of a roughly circular bank, which is now up to about 17 feet (5 metres) high but which must once have been of much greater proportion, enclosing an area of over 27 acres (11 hectares). The bank is cut by a ditch and originally, on the inner edge of the ditch, there stood almost 100 of the great, undressed, natural sarsens, each of which may have weighed as much as 50 tons. The enclosure is effectively cut into four quadrants by entrances and there are two more circles, the northern Cove and the Southern Inner Circle, within the main enclosure.

It is generally thought that the Avebury Stone Circle represented a social and/or religious centre for the primitive farming communities which had become established on the Wessex downland because of the open, well-drained nature of the land. Such land lent itself to the farming methods practised by the people who had moved into the area from the European continent, probably via the Ridgeway.

The Sanctuary

At Overton Hill, opposite the start of the Ridgeway, is the Sanctuary **10**, referred to briefly earlier, which authorities now consider would be more properly named Overton Hill Circles because of the four distinct phases of construction which seem to have taken place here.

The Sanctuary was the name given in 1720 by William Stukeley to two stone circles which stood at this point until 1724 when they were broken up. The antiquary, John Aubrey, also referred to this monument in 1648. The exact site of the stone circles was then lost, but it was recovered and excavated by M. E. and B. H. Cunnington in 1930. Rectangular concrete pillars have been used to mark the positions where stone holes have been found, while the six concentric rings of holes and the small central hole which once held wooden posts have been marked by round pillars. It has been suggested that the timber structures were replaced by the stone ones in the early Bronze Age when the West Kennett Avenue, linking Avebury with the Sanctuary, was also built.

It seems likely that the Sanctuary was erected for religious purposes and that the first quite small, rather flimsy hut was built on the site before 2500 B C during late Neolithic times, and that the rings of post holes represent successive phases of larger and more robust buildings perhaps completed more than 500 years later.

Long barrows

If you look almost due south from the Sanctuary, a long, tree-covered mound marks the site of another prehistoric site, East Kennett Long Barrow **11**. There is no public right of way to this site and the side ditches which once flanked the mound have now been ploughed over. No record exists to indicate that the barrow has been excavated, but it is almost certain that it is of the chambered type and similar to that of West Kennett Long Barrow **12** to the north-west of its eastern companion. These long barrows were chambered burial tombs which were in use for perhaps 1,000 years during late Neolithic times. In the case of the West Kennett Barrow, remains of at least 46 individuals who had been buried there have been uncovered during excavations of the site. The West Kennett site is well worth a visit now that it has been restored by the Department of the Environment, and access is via a track which leads from the A 4 about 1 mile (1.5 km) to the east of Beckhampton roundabout.

Sarsen stones

The word 'sarsen' is thought to have been derived from 'Saracen', and therefore sarsen or Saracen stones were believed to have been pagan monuments. In fact, these sometimes very large boulders of cemented sandstone which litter Fyfield Down are all that remains, after weathering and erosion, of a once continuous horizon of Tertiary sandstone that was deposited on the chalk.

A sidetrip into Fyfield Down National Nature Reserve is worthwhile. English Nature has erected an information board by the Ridgeway at the point where it is joined by the Herepath from Avebury; there are a number of paths through the Nature Reserve.

A sarsen on the Avenue at Avebury.

2 Ogbourne St George to Fox Hill

past Snap and Liddington Castle
7½ miles (11.9 km)

From Ogbourne St George **9** you can choose to rejoin the Ridgeway by the A345 at Southend or return to the point where you left the route of the Ridgeway to turn left into the village. There you continue straight on, as indicated by the Ridgeway signpost, and dive into a tree-lined and partly sunken lane which can be quite muddy following wet weather. As it continues, a little to the east of south, the going can remain rather muddy underfoot. It then ascends and, as it does, the lane becomes less sunken so that the village of Ogbourne St George can be seen to the left across the valley. After a little over 800 yards (730 metres) the Ridgeway takes a sharp turn to the left, and descends gently towards the road at the hamlet of Southend, the track becoming partially gravelled as you approach the houses, and then metalled. To the right of the road, an attractive collection of buildings comes into view. Some of these are part timbered and thatched, and look, at first sight, to be authentically Tudor. The road crosses a small bridge over the River Og, continues straight ahead, and crosses the busy A345 road. Once over the road, you will find that the owner of the cottage facing the Ridgeway about 50 yards along on your right has provided a water tap on his front wall for thirsty travellers.

Once again, the track becomes a grassy sunken lane and gently climbs the hill. In about 440 yards it passes between the brick abutments of a former bridge which once carried a railway line, now a traffic-free cycle route, from Chiseldon over the path; here the route bears slightly east. The incline gradually steepens as you approach a ridge and the route begins to head in a more north-easterly direction. By a newish house, the way crosses the Roman road which, as usual, runs arrow-straight and which, a little further north, provides the line for part of the A345 road from Chiseldon.

To the left of the track a little further along, there is a wind pump and reservoir alongside some chalk pits. As the path continues to climb on to the ridge, the trees which obscured the scenery thin out and there are panoramic views to the north and west. A few hundred yards past the wind pump the slope gradually begins to ease as you approach the brow of the ridge.

To the right, on the map, the names Yielding Copse, the intriguing Oak Stagger and other 'copses' identify the various small woods in the area.

A path joins from the left and shortly, at the crossing of the ways, where there is another reservoir, the Ridgeway turns sharply to the left (north). Your route is clearly marked, however, and by now you have reached the height of 780 feet (237 metres), providing more panoramic views, including, for the first time on the route, some woodlands.

The way is broader now, and quite level. There are slight undulations along the lane and the views, to the golf course and beyond, are still pleasant.

Approaching Chase Wood and Round Hill Downs, there is a rather ancient and rusting water tower which might perhaps have stored water from an underground spring to give a head of pressure for the buildings nearby. Turn left here on to the metalled farm road. This soon crosses the Aldbourne–Ogbourne St George road (called 'Copse Drove') and then you are on a green lane once again. In the flat fields to the right of the

Contours are given in metres
The vertical interval is 5m

way, cereal crops may show green in April and, among them, the ground is thick with flinty shards and nodules. Flints protrude from the track, too, as I discovered once when I tripped over one! In this area there is a layer of clay with flint overlying the chalk.

This lane continues northwards for some $1\frac{1}{2}$ miles ($2\frac{1}{2}$ km) with bluebells and primroses showing in the undergrowth during spring. About half a mile (1 km) beyond the metalled road, there is a crossing of the ways where the map marks a trig point, but a signpost tells you to continue on. The track to the left heads towards a mast and to the right leads to the abandoned village of Snap **13** (see page 47). There are also signs of a small underground reservoir here. On these dry, chalk ridges of the Wessex Downs, water has always been in short supply – perhaps the ancients made use of dew ponds? (See page 45.) Ahead, between the descent and the ascent to the slopes of Liddington Castle Fort **14**, there are fine views to the east and west.

Near the beginning of the slopes which eventually lead up to the hill fort, the Ridgeway changes from a byway to a bridleway and you go through a gate. To the right of the track, which hugs the fenceline, there is a clearly defined linear earthwork as you approach the fort which lies to the left and commands the heights of Liddington Hill: 911 feet (277 metres) at its summit, the highest point along the Ridgeway. As the ascent eases, the actual castle ramparts project slightly above the top of the hill. It must once have been a peaceful place, and it is still lovely with a sense of real height and isolation, but the noise from the M4 motorway tends to disturb the quiet.

Liddington Castle, which is marked by a trig point, is just a short diversion from the Ridgeway and can be approached by a permissive path (not shown on the map) leading around the edge of the field. This path follows the fenceline to the left of the gateway where the Ridgeway bears right away from the Castle.

From the castle, the growing conurbation of Swindon can be seen to the north. The castle provides a good view of the lowlands all around and it is not hard to imagine why it was chosen as the site for a defensive earthwork. On the trig point is a plaque celebrating the fact that Liddington Hill was beloved by nationally known Victorian authors, Richard Jefferies, a farmer's son, and Alfred Williams, a Swindon railway worker.

Pit
(dis)
202
Liddington Castle △ 277
Fort 14
Liddington
Hill
267

Pillow
Mound

Long
Barrow

222
MS

209

Tumulus

276

79

Earthwork

270

Folly
Barn

255

Earthwork

200

Earthwork

190

180

BS

78

Upham Farm
Cottages

Lower Upham
Farm

Earthwork

Ridgeway

Earthwork

260

Shipley Bottom

Cumulus

Cumuli

185

200

240

230

250

Medieval Village of Upham
(site of)

Upha
Cops

Reservoir

Upham Hall

Upper Upham

253

77

Earthwork

Medieval Village of Snap
(site of)

Mast

261

Reservoir

Reservoir

Snap 13

Wd Pp

Whitefield
Hill

260

Snap Farm
Snap Farm Cottages

Woodsend

Tom's Rosetta

249

250

76

Field System

255

236

Cheldene

Earthwork

245

Cumulus

260

21

22

Contours are given in metres
The vertical interval is 5m

43

Leaving Liddington Hill, the Ridgeway veers from north to north-east. The track now descends towards the B4192 and the M4, and from the point at which the path meets the B4192 it follows roads for about 1¼ miles (2 km). When you reach the B4192, turn left on to it, heading towards Swindon. This can be a busy road, but the broad verge provides a safe place to walk or ride. In a short distance, take the road to the right signposted to Little Hinton and Bourton. Soon after the turning to Manor Farm, the road passes over the M4 motorway – a chance, after more leisurely journeying, to reflect upon the pros and cons of motorised transport. The landmark to aim for is the radio mast at the top of Fox Hill, although you do not, in fact, arrive precisely at its foot. As you walk along the road, you will pass by the obliquely situated Front Lodge Cottages which stand guard to the entrance drive of King Edward's Place and, shortly afterwards, you cross yet another Roman road which has been adopted by modern route planners, the Ermin Way. And here, most welcome at the appropriate time of day, is the Shepherd's Rest public house **15**. The landlord has kindly allowed a water trough to be placed behind the pub for thirsty dogs and horses. There is car parking further along at Fox Hill, and Wanborough is just 1½ miles away along the Ermin Way.

Wanborough
2 km or 1 mile

6 km or 3½ miles
B4192 Aldbourne

Contours are given in metres
The vertical interval is 5m

The origins of chalk

Most of the higher ground along which the Ridgeway makes its way consists of what is often described as Wessex chalk downland and the chalk hills of the Chilterns; for some reason, the latter countryside is referred to as downland only in some patches. Other National Trails, such as the South Downs Way, also follow the line of a chalk scarp. A glance at a simple geological map shows that much of south-eastern England is situated on chalk rock which runs, like a three-pronged fork with a short handle, from the Dorset coast to north Norfolk with the two southern tines separated by the Weald and meeting the sea via the North and South Downs. It is these well-drained chalk uplands that have been used as areas on which to farm and on which lines of communication could be established away from the forested, marshy and hostile lands in the valleys below.

Many people, if asked to describe chalk, might well name the white sticks once used so commonly to write on school blackboards. In fact, chemically, this is a different material from that which is the foundation of Ridgeway country. On the other hand, most people have quite a good idea of typical chalk scenery with its rolling hills, springy, close-cropped turf, beech woodlands or wide-open arable land. But what is the chalk on which the land has evolved?

It has long been known that, chemically, chalk is largely calcium carbonate, that is lime, so it will effervesce in contact with an acid such as hydrochloric. Sometimes chalk may be stained reddish brown or yellowish orange with iron, and sometimes it is punctuated with layers of oddly shaped siliceous flints, but essentially chalk is white in colour so that if the turf is removed to form, say, a giant horse shape on a hillside, the figure can be seen standing out white against green for miles around. Chalk is permeable to water and, when soaked, it can be soft and sticky; if it is dry it seems as hard as any other stone. Its permeability to water allows the soils which form on it, shallow though they may be, to drain well. In fact, one of the problems of life on chalk country is the lack of permanent sources of water. It is this feature which led local people to excavate the so-called dew ponds.

The 19th century journalist and Wiltshire countryman, Richard Jefferies, described the way in which local people constructed dew ponds in his day by digging out a shallow pit

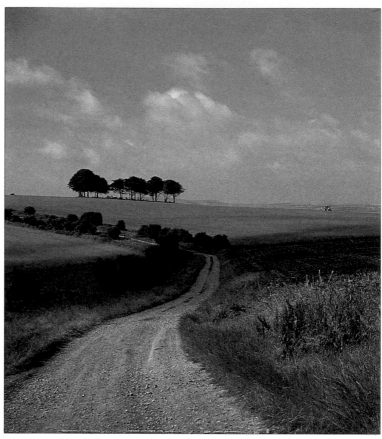

Chalk downland dominates the landscape of the western half of the Ridgeway.

over quite a large area. It would then be lined with impermeable clay, which had been mixed with soot to deter insects and worms from boring through it. As mist and low cloud condensed and any falling rain was captured, the pond would gradually fill with water. With natural waterways and springs in short supply high on the downs, these ponds were essential for stock in the days before a piped water supply was available.

In complete contrast to the general dryness of the chalk ridge, parts of the Ridgeway lie on fairly thick clay which overlies the chalk, especially on the hill tops. Examples are to be found in the Winterbourne Monkton Down/Hackpen Hill area, around the Wiltshire/Oxfordshire border near Bishopstone, and at Gramps Hill near Wantage. The clay-with-flints capping on the Chiltern escarpment causes similar conditions which can give rise to deep ruts which fill with water in winter; however, ongoing repairs are reducing such conditions on the Ridgeway.

It has also long been known that chalk must have formed as a sediment in the sea but it was once thought to have been deposited in deep oceans because, in some ways, it resembles certain oozes which form in such places. It is now understood, however, that the great thicknesses of chalk which underlie the landscape were laid down in warm, shallow, clear seas that spread across much of what is now northern Europe more than 65 million years ago. It was deposited as a very fine-grained, calcareous mud, made up largely of countless billions of tiny shells, shell fragments and the remains of some small plants called coccolithophorids. The tiny, calcareous shells are known as coccoliths. The flints which are so often found in the upper layers of chalk are made up of silica but their exact origin remains uncertain. It may be that the compound which comprises them has resulted from a kind of 'gel' made from the solution of fragments of the skeletons of sea sponges.

Snap Village

In contrast to the ancient monuments seen so far along the Ridgeway, the site of the old village of Snap **13** is a more poignant reminder of changes in rural life. Snap was a very old settlement, dating back at least to 1377 when it was mentioned in connection with the Poll Tax, but by the turn of this century there were only a dozen cottages and a farm in the village. Changes in farming practices in the area, from labour-intensive arable farming to stock grazing that requires fewer workers, had meant that the residents of Snap eventually had to move elsewhere to find jobs.

By 1905 Snap was abandoned, although the farm itself lingered on to the 1930s. Now the outlines of the village can be seen best in the winter, although sarsen rubble marks the remains of the cottages. Sites abandoned in the 20th century are rare, and Snap is unique in Wiltshire; its story is outlined in a monograph published by the Wiltshire Library and Museum Service.

Certainly it is a good place to ponder about the current changes in rural life – will settlements be similarly deserted in the future, or will they survive? Compare Snap's fate with that of the villages of Lockinge and Ardington (see page 74) further along the Ridgeway – both have lessons for the future.

3 Fox Hill to Whitehorse Hill

past Ashbury and Uffington Castle
5½ miles (8.7 km)

From the crossroads and the Shepherd's Rest **15**, continue on the road, gently uphill and bearing slightly left, until after about 200 yards (180 metres) the Ridgeway bears right and north-east becoming a broad track as it does so. There is ample car parking here. The surface of the Ridgeway from here to beyond Whitehorse Hill used to be deeply rutted in many places, but extensive repairs, funded by the Countryside Commission and the County Councils, have resulted in vastly improved conditions.

After about 275 yards another track crosses the trail. On either side, the fields are open, arable land, and the map suggests that there are more reservoirs. From the path, looking to the north, the reservoir in front of the 832-foot (253-metre) summit and trig point of Charlbury Hill are apparent. To the right (south) is the open, rounded high ground of Lammy Down where, once again, there is a reservoir. There are ancient field systems and strip lynchets marked on the map on the Bishopstone side of the hills to the north, but these are not visible from the path. A lynchet or 'linch' is the line of a ridge marking the boundary of a prehistoric field, and was caused by soil slipping downhill as a result of ploughing, forming a ridge along the lower boundary of the field.

The Ridgeway first descends and then rises gently towards Ridgeway Farm, where a minor road from the village of Bishopstone **16**, about a mile (1.5 km) to the north, crosses the route. Part of the way down the hill towards Ridgeway Farm, a farm track joins the Ridgeway from the left and another leaves to the right 100 yards further on. At the foot of the descent, another major right of way crosses the route which, in a northerly direction, also leads to Bishopstone; this track goes through the deep cut in the land visible from the Ridgeway.

Look from the path towards Charlbury Hill, mentioned earlier, in a direction which would now be just about due west, for traces of those ancient field systems. To the south and east, the countryside is open, gently rolling, with isolated lines and clumps of trees here and there, while to the north and west the land falls away more steeply to the flatter country around Bishopstone.

Contours are given in metres
The vertical interval is 5m

5 km or 3 miles
Baydon

49

Clearly signposted, the way takes you straight on and, for a short stretch at least, the walking is comparatively level. After less than 400 yards of easy going, the broad track begins to rise gently and, on both sides, the countryside is prairie-like, although there are some lines of trees to the south and west to break the monotony. About half a mile (1 km) beyond the road and Ridgeway Farm, you step out of Wiltshire and into Oxfordshire, the boundary being marked by a wooden post. From here to Idstone Hill, the map tells you that you have climbed a mere 66 feet (20 metres) but, on the ground, the ascent seems to be greater. Where the partly metalled and partly chalk-surfaced road crosses, continue to the north-east. There are farm buildings at the crossing, and drinking water can be had from a tap a short distance off the Ridgeway down the track to the left. The way now levels out once again.

Looking to right and left, as the path winds up between the trees, I found myself in April reflecting sadly on the prairie-style, monoculture farming. Perhaps as little as thirty years ago, the path would probably have been bounded by early spring flowers, but these have now given way to crops and pesticides in the interests of economy and efficiency and to provide consumers with cheap produce. Formerly this stretch of the path was very rutted, but repairs have made the going easy. The deep layer of clay here masks the effects of the chalk which elsewhere lies near the surface and gives rise to a profusion of calcicolous plants. Here the paucity of flowers and associated animal life produced a rather dull and strangely quiet atmosphere, although oilseed rape, which takes the place of cereals these days, was just beginning to flower. And by the side of the path, from time to time, could be seen the tiny blue flowers of that charming little plant, the speedwell.

About an hour after leaving Fox Hill some 3 miles (5 km) behind, you arrive at the crossing of the B4000 road to Ashbury **17** where Ashbury Folly is marked on the map. However, if you are coming from the west and thinking of going into Ashbury, you may prefer to use the footpath which goes off to the left at the previous field boundary about half a mile before the road junction, rather than the 'B' road. All that is left of the folly is a little copse of trees. Ashbury, once praised as the best-kept village in England, is a little over half a mile (1 km) downhill along the road to the north-west. Anyone completing the western half of the Ridgeway in two days, as I have done, will find this a convenient stopping place. The path crosses the

B4000 Lambourn
9 km or 5½ miles

Contours are given in metres
The vertical interval is 5m

51

B4000 marching steadily north-eastwards, towards the ancient monument of Wayland's Smithy.

A little over 400 yards further on, a grassy farm track leads off to the left; the corner is marked on the map as Kingstone Barn but there is no trace here now of a barn which disappeared some time ago. And in another 400 yards there is a line of trees astride the Ridgeway. You are now beginning to climb again and then the way continues to be fringed with still more trees. After another 300 yards a track leads to Odstone Barn which, this time, is still standing. About 300 yards beyond this point, you come upon the path off to the left to Wayland's Smithy Long Barrow **18**, partly hidden among the trees. It is well worth a look and, on a rather bleak and wintry day, it feels a lonely place and few people would fail to be carried back in time (see page 57).

A CIRCULAR WALK TO ASHDOWN HOUSE AND WAYLAND'S SMITHY

7¾ miles (12.5 km)

Beginning at the car park where Ashbury Hill crosses the Ridgeway, walk along the Ridgeway in a south-westerly direction. In about 200 yards, at the next crossing of tracks, turn left towards Red Barn and follow the track as it skirts to the west of Hailey Wood, Middle Wood and Upper Wood. Ashdown House **22** can be seen to the left of the track in Ashdown Park past Middle Wood. Built in the late 1600s. it was described by Pevsner as the 'perfect doll's house', and one can see why. It is now owned by the National Trust and is open from April to the end of October, on Wednesday and Saturday afternoons only. The woods are open all year, except Fridays.

Continue southwards past the end of Upper Wood for about 220 yards and take the path to the left. At the next crossing of tracks turn left again. Turn left on to the road and, after about half a mile (1 km), almost opposite a road leading to Ashdown Farm, strike right across the field and up Weathercock Hill. Follow the path, initially due east and then north-east, until a crossing of tracks, then turn left and continue back to the Ridgeway. Turn left again and, passing Wayland's Smithy **18** on the right, continue along the Ridgeway back to the car park. A leaflet giving further details of this walk is included in the *Ridgeway Routes Pack* (see page 141).

Contours are given in metres
The vertical interval is 5m

Between the Smithy and Knighton Hill, less than 400 yards to the north-east along the Ridgeway, another line of trees nears the track, and Whitehorse Hill **20** with the ramparts of Uffington Castle **19** hill fort come into view. At the road, Wayland's Smithy is clearly signposted, as is the Ridgeway in both directions. Simply cross the road and continue along the broad track towards Whitehorse Hill which seems to dominate the view ahead.

The ascent from the road at Knighton Hill begins gently at first. The fort ridge terminating in the scarp of Uffington Hill cuts across the Ridgeway path in front of you. About 600 yards before reaching Uffington Castle itself, the Ridgeway passes yet another road/track. This leads north to the National Trust car park and south to Lambourn (about 5 miles/8 km away). The trail now steepens, taking you from about 680 feet (207 metres) to just over 820 feet (250 metres), a climb of some 140 feet (43 metres) in just over half a mile (under 1 km). The Ridgeway soon passes to the south of Uffington Castle, situated on land owned by the National Trust. Near the bottom of the slope there is access over a stile and just after you reach the top of the hill, there is a gate which leads to the ramparts of the castle where the trig point for Whitehorse Hill is clearly visible, although the horse itself is over the brow of the hill.

Do make the short diversion to the castle's ramparts – it is well worth it. Like many of the hill forts, Uffington Castle has a rich and varied flora, despite the thousands of feet trampling all over it! The ramparts support orchids, candytuft and field fleawort, in addition to the more common chalk downland species. The trackside verge of the Ridgeway itself has, from late spring to early autumn, a profusion of flowers, such as orchids, hay rattle, scabious, knapweed, several species of vetch, and a variety of grasses. Many of these are particularly attractive to butterflies. Chalkhill Blue, Small Blue, Gatekeeper, Ringlet and Marbled White can all be found in this area.

Although the ramparts of Uffington Castle are now much eroded, there is still evidence of an outer bank, a ditch and an inner bank. From the trig point the views all around, but especially to the north, are spectacular.

The White Horse **21** can be reached by making for the thorn bushes to the north of the trig point, then bearing right along the contour path. The hill figure is just below the signs asking you to avoid walking on it – there has been much unnecessary erosion in recent years. From the top, the shape is not readily discernible – you need to go a mile or two to the north and look back! But the magnificent contours of The Manger, nestling beneath the horse's head, are clearly visible – a truly splendid example of a dry valley formed by a melting glacier in the Ice Ages. To return to the Ridgeway, either double back to the hill fort or, if you do not mind missing out a hundred yards or so of the Ridgeway, go eastwards to the field boundary, and then follow it southwards to a stile in the corner. On the other side is the Ridgeway.

The villages of Uffington and Woolstone lie to the north of Whitehorse Hill and there are car parks on Woolstone Hill and at the foot of Uffington Castle (for the disabled and elderly only).

Contours are given in metres
The vertical interval is 5m

The Iron Age hill forts

One of the most notable features of a journey along the Ridgeway is the line of earthworks, above all Barbury Castle **6**, Liddington **14**, Uffington **19** and Segsbury **29**, which occupy prominent points of high ground especially on the Wessex ridge.

The official plaque briefly informing visitors to Uffington Castle of its origins and history describes it as a '. . . hill fort defended by a bank and ditch with an entrance on the west and built during the Iron Age, 300 BC to AD 43'. It is obviously very hard to date a structure such as a hill fort. One way is by dating artefacts, such as tools, weapons or pottery which might be uncovered during excavation of the structure. So, if you find something which is clearly of Iron Age origin in the ditch which forms part of the castle defences, you know that the ditch must have been there first because an object cannot be deposited in something which does not exist! On the other hand, you do not know how long the structure had been there *before* the object was deposited in it. But, if no earlier objects are found, then it seems reasonable to assume that the structure must be more or less contemporaneous with what you have found.

As J. R. L. Anderson points out, however, common sense would suggest that all the hill forts along the Ridgeway were elements of a common strategic, defensive structure and that their location must mean that their original purpose was to defend the Ridgeway – an important line of communication – against attack from the north. As he goes on to suggest, such a tactic would have required considerable organisation and strong leadership. This would have been hard to find during the Iron Age period preceding the arrival of the Romans. There was, however, an earlier culture capable of organisation on such a scale. During the Bronze Age people would have no reason to defend the Ridgeway from the south but they *could* have had a need to defend it from unknown marauders from the' north in much the same way that, in later times, the Romans built Hadrian's Wall to defend their colony against attack from the untamed lands in Scotland.

Of course, once such structures have been built, they obviously do not fall overnight and it is quite possible that people of a later age made use of them. J. R. L. Anderson's view does seem to make more strategic and political sense than the theory which stems from simple archaeological investigation.

Uffington Castle, one of the many Iron Age hill forts along the Ridgeway.

Perhaps we shall never know which argument is correct but it may be that, as dating methods improve, the truth will emerge. In the meantime, however, it is enough to marvel at the skill and effort that went into building fortresses that are still evident today, more than 2,000 years later.

Wayland's Smithy 18

The plaque in front of the barrow describes it as a Neolithic burial chamber in a long barrow edged with stones, built in about 2800 BC. Beneath the mound was found a smaller long barrow of an earlier date with burials in wooden chambers. On either side of the Smithy is a ditch marked by lines of trees. The main entrance cairn is marked by four large stones. Wayland was the magical smith god of the Saxons and local legend has it that, if you leave your horse, together with a suitable payment, by the tomb, the animal will have been reshod on your return the next day. But Saxon gods would not have been heard of here until more than 3,000 years after the barrow was built. Access to Wayland's Smithy is easy from Compton Beauchamp and Knighton via Knighton Hill.

4 Whitehorse Hill to Wantage

via Sparsholt Firs
6¼ miles (10.2 km)

Note that the distance given above is from the summit of Whitehorse Hill and Uffington Castle to the point where the Ridgeway route crosses Manor Road, which leads northwards into the town of Wantage. Anyone staying in Wantage or planning to make use of its facilities will have a road walk of just over 2 miles (about 3.5 km) into the town, although the Court Hill Ridgeway Centre, which is a youth hostel with camping, is only 440 yards off the ridge down the same road.

Returning to the Ridgeway route from Uffington Castle **19** (and nearby car parks), and keeping the castle on your left-hand side, the way now takes you a little north of east and begins slowly to descend from the hill's highest point of 859 feet (261 metres) and, as you look ahead, the going seems to be undulating. On the south-eastern horizon, beyond a clump of trees, a radio mast rises up to provide an indication of the way ahead; in fact, the mast is about 440 yards off the path to the south. The line of trees which leads off from the Ridgeway, about 880 yards east of the summit of Whitehorse Hill, is known, for obvious reasons, as Long Plantation. Shortly after passing the plantation, the track begins to climb again and, a little further on, the rounded hill to the south of the way, known as Rams Hill, is indicated on the map as the site of yet another fort, but the plough seems to have removed all traces of it so far as can be seen from the Ridgeway. There are wide views to the north, with Uffington and Kingston Lisle lying on the plain.

A CIRCULAR WALK FROM SPARSHOLT FIRS

7¾ miles (12.5 km) (see maps on pages 59 and 61)

From the car park at Sparsholt Firs **26** on the B4001, cross the road and walk westwards along the Ridgeway past Blowingstone Hill **23** to Whitehorse Hill **20** itself. Just past the trig point to the right of the Castle off the Ridgeway, turn sharp left up to Uffington Down. The so-called Cross Dyke here has, through ploughing over hundreds of years, become a sort of shallow man-made scarp and then a raised causeway which marks the parish boundary. With gallops to the left, at the apex of a

Contours are given in metres
The vertical interval is 5m

triangular shaped line of trees, follow the track to the left and then right. A track then turns to the left although the gallops continue southwards; take this towards Crog Hill. At Crog Hill follow the track to the right and take the next left as far as the minor road. Turn right on to the road and walk past Sevenbarrows House on the right. Just past Lambourn Seven Barrows, take the track to the left and follow it until it emerges on to the B4001. Turn left and follow the road back to the car park.

Having passed Rams Hill, the track begins to swing south-wards and before the next hill ahead can be seen the road leading to Kingston Lisle, about three-quarters of a mile (1.25 km) to the north down Blowingstone Hill **23**. There is an 800-yard walk down the road to look at the Blowing Stone in the garden of a cottage. If one blows into one of the holes which pierce the stone, one can produce a deep, trumpet-like sound. King Alfred may have put it to use during the Battle of Ashdown.

From the Ridgeway, and situated just to the south of the village, can be seen Kingstone Lisle House **24**, a fine Georgian house set in parkland.

The road which the Ridgeway crosses at this point joins the B4001 in the south and, in about 5 miles (8 km), leads to the village of Lambourn. About 2½ miles (4 km) from the Ridgeway, down the road towards Lambourn, is the spectacular group of tumuli known as the Seven Barrows **25**, although there must have been something like thirty different kinds of barrows here before farming took its toll. Even now, more than seven are visible. To the south of the Ridgeway, the views now are rather restricted but do include the attractive rolling downland which typifies this part of Oxfordshire. The top of the hill is reached at a height of 743 feet (226 metres) and, to the right of the track, there is a group of trees called Hillbarn Clump, sadly devastated by the 1990 storms. Between Collett Bush and Wixen Bush the track climbs. The profusion of chalk-loving plants here will delight the summer visitor. This area is one of five along the western half of the Ridgeway being managed, with the help of Ridgeway Volunteers, to maintain the chalk flowers and insects. The track runs south-eastwards again, climbing to a height of some 794 feet (242 metres) before it levels out.

Soon after a track to the right leads to Hill Barn; there is a drinking water tap at this junction. You are now approaching Sparsholt Firs **26**, which, despite their name, seem to consist almost entirely of deciduous trees. Just before you arrive at the plantation itself, the Ridgeway route joins a metalled road from Sparsholt 1½ miles (2.4 km) to the north. Bear right on to the road and, where it joins the B4001, continue straight ahead on to the broad Ridgeway track. To the south of the track, looking back a little, are the Lambourn Downs, and on the north of the path adjacent to the gallops there is a highly favoured area for flying model aircraft. By all means stop and watch from the Ridgeway, but please note that this is private land – the model aircraft club has permission to use the gallops.

Kingston Lisle House

Blowing Stone

The Warren

24

Blowingstone Hill

23

The Rides

Quarry (dis)

Kingstonhill Barn

203

Reservoir

226

86

Hillbarn Clump

206

215

210

205

200

195

Tumulus

Oakbank Plantations

Seven Acre

B 4507

MS

123

Oakbank Barn

Sparsholt Field

Field Barn

Sheephouse Bottom

Clem Cotta

202

Collett Bush

Wixen Bush

235 △ 236

Rubblepit Plantation

242

Pit (dis)

Old Plantation

Reservoir Hill Barn

244

Down Barn

Sparsholt Firs

26

P

200

210

201

85

190

185

180

175

170

Gallops

Scary Hill

172

Sparsholt Down

Moss Hill

Radio Station

Mast

234

Sparsholt Firs

Pit (dis)

Tumulus

226

84

Eastmanton Down

Gallop

Quarry (dis)

Crog Hill

Westcot Down

Tumuli

Tumulus

Co Const Bdy

Long Barrow

Tumuli

BS

153

Tumulus

Pit (dis)

Tumulus

Pit Down

Old Warren

Boundary Covert

214

219

83

Seven Barrows

25

32

Sevenbarrows House

Tumuli

Road Down

B 4001

34

Contours are given in metres
The vertical interval is 5m

61

The countryside in this area is open and pleasing, with panoramic views in most directions. You travel south-eastwards at first, passing another Hackpen Hill to the left, and then, as the way bears eastwards again, a line of racehorse gallops accompanies the route for about a mile (1.5 km). The unploughed, formerly rabbit-cropped turf of these areas is now carefully managed by private owners to provide large gallops with soft, springy turf on which to train racehorses, with little fear of injury to these highly bred and very expensive animals.

On the right just over the brow of the hill is Folly Clump. This small spinney of beech trees originally planted to commemorate races won by an owner's racehorse was replanted a few years ago by a local trainer.

Through the valley to the north-east can be seen the village of Letcombe Bassett **27** about half a mile (1 km) north of the Ridgeway. If, at Gramp's Hill **28**, you look back in the direction from which you have just come, the natural cut into the hillside, known as the Devil's Punchbowl, can clearly be seen. Cross the road and continue on the more or less level track. Any views from here are restricted by hedges and small trees. About 880 yards after leaving the road, a track leads off to the right, and

Contours are given in m
The vertical interval is

passes Parsonagehill Barn. Shortly after, a metalled track to the left, known as Smith's Hill, leads down to the Letcombes – the way to the right, however, is private. In about 100 yards there is another footpath heading downhill to the left, to Letcombe Bassett (made famous as Cresscombe in Thomas Hardy's *Jude the Obscure*), which is about half a mile (1 km) to the north.

Now the Ridgeway begins to descend towards what appears on the map as the major earthwork of Segsbury or Letcombe Castle **29** fort to the north of the track. Opposite Segsbury Farm, a broad track is shown as a right of way to the fort. The Castle has been entered into the Countryside Stewardship Scheme and is now being farmed in a traditional way. The scrub on the banks and in the ditch has been cleared to reveal the structure of the fort and sheep are grazing the whole area. From here, continue roughly eastwards until you reach Manor Road which leads left down into Wantage.

For anyone continuing onwards, the signposts clearly indicate that you turn right on to the road and almost immediately left. Notice, however, that the Court Hill Ridgeway Centre **30** (see page 64) is signposted as a quarter of a mile (400 metres) to the left down Manor Road towards Wantage.

urs are given in metres
vertical interval is 5m

The Ridgeway Centre offers accommodation and field studies facilities.

The Ridgeway Centre

It may perhaps seem a little unusual to be including in a guide book to a rural national trail a special feature devoted to a residential facility which the trail offers but this is rather a unique situation.

Described in the official leaflet as '. . . a lively and exciting place to stay . . .' and located on Court Hill with fine views across the Vale of White Horse, the Ridgeway Centre **30** makes an ideal rest stop. The accommodation and other facilities have been developed around five disused barns from local farms that were dismantled and re-erected on the present site, which was originally a chalk pit and became the Wantage rubbish tip. The site has now a new lease of life and the Centre has a holiday flat, a display and field studies area, a camping site, a barbecue area, the usual kitchen and dining room and superior grade and standard grade youth hostel accommodation with four-berth cabins as well as dormitories.

The Centre was sponsored mainly by the Vale of White Horse District Council, Countryside Commission, Thames and Chilterns Tourist Board, Ernest Cook Trust, Wantage Town Council, Oxfordshire County Council and the Toby Adcock Memorial Fund. These organisations should be congratulated for their far-sightedness in promoting such a centre. Dr Dick Squires, a local GP, also deserves a mention. Having thought of the idea of a hostel on the Downs, he set about raising the funds and was involved in the project from start to finish.

Anyone wishing to stay at the Centre or to make enquiries about the facilities mentioned here, as well as a variety of others, should contact the Warden, The Court Hill Ridgeway Centre, Court Hill, Letcombe Regis, Wantage, Oxfordshire, tel. Wantage (01235) 760253.

5 Wantage to Bury Down

past the Baron of Wantage Monument and Scutchamer Knob
5¾ miles (9.2 km)

It is worth bearing in mind that, if you have decided to stay the night in Wantage itself, unless you take a taxi to rejoin the Ridgeway, in the morning you will have a 2-mile (3.5-km) road walk uphill before you get back to the route. There is limited car parking at Manor Road, however.

Crossing Manor Road, turn right and immediately left to resume your eastward journey. The countryside on either side of the Ridgeway is still typical of modern farming methods although the view to the south, through the hedgerow, is much pleasanter.

The route begins to climb upwards a little after you pass a row of houses to the south, including a recently converted barn. Over the hill, and down again; the metalling on the track begins to peter out while the views ahead to the east start to open up. Pass the buildings of Whitehouse Farm on your left.

At the point where the track takes a sharp turn to the left (north) there is a small coniferous plantation edged by some young beech trees. After about 100 yards you come to a T-junction.

The Ridgeway turns sharply to the south-east here but for travellers from the east, another sign indicates a short cut to Court Hill Ridgeway Centre **30**. The way now becomes the typical, broad, rutted, chalky grass track pointing in the direction of a radio mast head. The shape of the hill here is such that the views to the north are somewhat restricted although, to the south-west, the broad expanses of open farmland, here and there dotted with patches of woodland, persist. Over the farmland, the tinkling songs of skylarks spiralling upwards mix with the occasional 'pee-wit' calls of the lapwings to add a little musical colour to the scene.

The B4494 road from Wantage comes into view but, before it is reached, the track forks. One is tempted to continue straight on to the south-east but the route follows the left-hand fork.

The Ordnance Survey map informs you that here, in 1872, bronze palstaves, which are axe heads designed to fit into split wooden handles, were found. Looking to the left, the views are mostly of arable fields with a point-to-point course just the other side of the road. I wonder what the Ridgeway was like when it was first being used as a trading route; with such farming methods in evidence and with modern roads in sight, too, it is hard to imagine, although this can be a good place to stop for coffee, sheltered by isolated trees and bushes. Somewhere, a hidden cock pheasant croaked out its harsh, unmusical call on a cold April day.

Approaching the road, the Ridgeway becomes a gravelled farm track once again and, at the crossing, there is ample car parking space. Simply cross the road and continue journeying

Contours are given in metres
The vertical interval is 5m

Furzewick Down is typical of the landscape to be seen on this section of the Ridgeway.

north-eastwards. Do not be tempted to take the metalled track forking left. In the distance, the spike of a monument comes into view, built 'on the Site of a Tumulus', according to the map. At this point, you are following part of the circular walk described on page 72, and to the left is Middlehill Down. The route is a broad grassy track and, in April 1988, when I first walked the route, I saw three hares playing in the fields to the right. Rather sadder, however, was a stained and battered notice dated 21st June 1987, 5 p.m. – apparently a cocker spaniel bitch had been lost, and I still wonder if she was ever found again. It was, though, a salutary warning for Ridgeway walkers to keep their dogs under control, especially as I heard the crack of shotguns.

From close to, the monument **31** looks smaller than it appears from the distance. On its square concrete plinth, the circular, concrete-cross-topped column of a monument to the soldier and Victoria Cross holder, Robert Loyd-Lindsay, Baron of Wantage, is hardly an attractive affair, erected as it was by the Baron's wife. On the other hand, as the tree cover begins to increase all around, the scenery gains interest and, from the density of hoofprints in the mud, this is obviously a popular route for horseriders.

In the late 19th century, Lord Wantage and his descendants planted a large number of scattered copses and shelterbelts, mainly of beech, elm and oak. In the present century, a phase of softwood planting brought the total area of woodland on the estate to about 1,000 acres (400 hectares). The contribution to the landscape made by this planting can readily be appreciated. The value of the woods for timber is supplemented by that of game rearing, and the land certainly creates the impression that it is well-husbanded, as partridges fly off from the long grass when you near a small plantation of conically shaped evergreens. The Ridgeway route bears slightly to the right with the curious little plantation on the left; other tracks here are 'Private, Keep Out'! A little to the east of the plantation by Ridgeway Down, there is a drinking water tap on the left-hand edge of the way. Also to the left is another curious stand of trees, this time circular, to the north of which is Midsummer Wood and Ardington Down. With the broad track climbing gently, and with very comfortable going underfoot, the route takes a slight turn to the north and, about 275 yards past the tap, the circular walk (see page 72) bears off sharply to the right, descending between two woods.

As you reach the brow of the hill, to the left of the Ridgeway there is an odd-looking, fenced square construction, which I suspect was a reservoir. After this, another plantation stands on the left and there are tracks crossing to left and right before it. Behind the fence on the north-west corner of this junction will be found a small sarsen stone bearing a plaque in memory of Lady Penelope Betjeman, wife of Sir John, the late Poet Laureate. The Betjemans lived at various times at Uffington, Wantage and Farnborough, often walking the Ridgeway, and in Farnborough Church there is a window to Betjeman by John Piper. From here, you can reach the villages of Lockinge and Ardington **32** about 2½ miles (4 km) to the north (see page 74).

It was here on the Ridgeway that a seemingly endless stream of motorcyclists passed me as they rode in the opposite direction to mine. At first, I was irritated by their presence but it must be admitted that they had as much right to be there as I did, and each of them could not have been more considerate. Shortly after the woodland, there is another path to the left, heading for East Ginge, from where East Hendred can be reached if you fancy a 3-mile (5-km) hike out of your way.

Approaching the top of the hill, with its stand of pine trees to the right, in the distance to the north of east the rather untidy sprawl of Harwell Business Centre and the Rutherford Appleton Laboratory come into view.

Contours are given in metres
The vertical interval is 5m

To the left now is East Ginge Down, and ahead is the top of Cuckhamsley Hill at 668 feet (203 metres), picked out by a stand of trees. On reaching them, I saw they were surrounded by a broken fence and marked 'Private', although the landowner has provided a stile leading into the trees. I could discern in a clearing among the trees what is marked on the map only as 'tumulus' but which is Scutchamer Knob **33**. It is a curious affair. It looks as though once it may have been a round barrow but it now is a semi-circular bank with no front. It appears to have been vandalised by those who evidently believed it held a hoard of treasure.

Opinions seem to differ as to the name 'Scutchamer'. It may have been derived from Cwicchelmshlaew, the burial place of the Saxon king, Cwicchelm, who died in AD 593, but Anderson claims that a 'scutcher' was someone who 'scutched' or beat out the flax after it had been retted or soaked to loosen the fibres, and that this was the place where local villagers once came to hold their fairs.

Conours are given in metres
The vertical interval is 5m

Continue onwards, past a crossing, and again there are gallops to the right. After another ½ mile or so, two more rights of way lead off to the left, the first to the north passing by the perimeter of Harwell Business Centre and the second heading north-east to Chilton. Your way continues straight ahead, a little to the south of east, with the Chilton Downs to the left, Cow Down to the right, and your destination for this section of the route, Bury Down, straight ahead. The views to the north are broad and sweeping. On your left now, the A34 trunk road strides, a broad, grey stripe across the green downland with Didcot Power Station on its left.

Didcot Power Station was built on the site of an old Army Central Ordnance Depot and cost £100 million to build. The first unit came into operation in 1970, and it now has four 500-megawatt generators driven by solid fuel. Most power stations of comparable size have eight of the giant cooling towers which make Didcot such a landmark but here there are only six, apparently to '. . . minimise their impact on the surrounding area . . .' Be that as it may, in certain lights the towers do have a kind of eerie charm. Interestingly, too, part of the site has been turned into a field study centre and nature trail for children.

On Bury Down **34**, where there is ample car parking space, the Ridgeway crosses a minor road leading in a southerly direction to the village of West Ilsley **35**. To the north, in about half a mile (1 km), the road joins the busy A34.

A CIRCULAR WALK TO SCUTCHAMER KNOB

6 miles (10 km) (see maps on pages 70 and 71)

Start at the car park where the B4494, Chainhill Road from Wantage, crosses the Ridgeway. Follow the Ridgeway eastwards past the monument **31** and Scutchamer Knob **33** to the point past Cuckhamsley Hill where the minor road from East Hendred reaches the Ridgeway. Here turn right as directed on to the circular walk and follow the walk past gallops on the left. Continue on the circular walk until it swings back to rejoin the Ridgeway between Wether Down and Ridgeway Down. Turn left and return to the car park.

Scutchamer Knob, the trees have subsequently been cleared.

Contours are given in metres
The vertical interval is 5m

Lockinge and Ardington

The abandonment of the hamlet of Snap (see page 47) is a salutary reminder of what can happen to a country village when there are no jobs for the residents. The same fate could have befallen the villages of Lockinge and Ardington **32**, near Wantage. Their population fell drastically after 1950 since the Lockinge Estate, both employer and landowner, was unable to provide enough jobs on its increasingly mechanised farmland.

Then in the early 1970s, Christopher Loyd, the estate owner, and his agent decided to do something practical to save the villages. Redundant farm buildings were used to house small businesses and craft workshops, which provide more than 100 jobs for residents of the area, and a village housing trust has renovated old cottages and built new homes, particularly for the elderly and young people, both of whom usually lose out in the village housing market. A local enterprise scheme links Ardington and Lockinge with three neighbouring villages, so the efforts in one area can spread further afield. Instead of becoming a backwater of decaying houses, or a commuter's oasis totally depopulated except at weekends, the villages are facing a more certain future and are unlikely to become the Snaps of the 21st century.

The memorial to Lord Wantage (1832–1901), who built a model farm and village on the Lockinge estate.

Today the Home Farm houses a craft centre as well as other small businesses.

6 Bury Down to Streatley

past Compton and Aldworth
8¼ miles (13.4 km)

This part of the Ridgeway is popular with walkers, horseriders and cyclists in all seasons and in all weathers. It is somehow encouraging to think that it is still a busy green road even if its use is for pleasure rather than necessity. And there is good countryside to the north-east with rolling, open downland and the occasional clump of trees breaking up the line of the horizon. From here to Streatley is just about my favourite stretch of the western Ridgeway but there is just one feature which mars this end of its length: it seems impossible to escape the traffic noise from the A34. Most of us use roads such as this one very regularly and, as we speed along, insulated from most of the engine and tyre noise, we scarcely think of the disturbance to the countryside and its inhabitants. Nevertheless, busy roads do have their advantages for some kinds of wildlife; kestrels, for example, seem to favour them as happy hunting grounds.

Before reaching the A34, a public right of way to West Ilsley **35** leaves the Ridgeway in a southerly direction; it is part of West Berkshire Council's recreational route (see page 78) and is well waymarked.

Even though you have crossed roads earlier along the Ridgeway, somehow it seems odd to be approaching such a major arterial road as the A34. The route to take is clearly indicated, however, by red arrows and acorn marker posts, and you are led on to a gravel track and a concrete tunnel which passes beneath the road. At this point, you are about 1½ miles (2.5 km) from East Ilsley; there is, in fact, a public right of way heading southwards from here, too. It is also possible to get to East Ilsley **36** via a number of tracks, particularly where the route bears a little more to the south and approaches to within just over a mile (1.75 km) of the centre of the village, which was once famous for its sheep fairs (see page 84).

With the A34 left behind, and with an easterly wind blowing, the noise from the road becomes less intrusive. Immediately you emerge from the tunnel, decorated with a mural by the local Compton Art Group, you bear right and then left, where, after another 100 yards, a gallop on your right runs southwards into the downs and woodlands.

A34(T) Didcot
7 km or 4½ miles

Chilton Downs

Grim's Ditch

Tile Barn

Ridgeway

P

Bury Down **34**

Gore Hill Farm

MS

84

84

Berkshire Circular Route

The Ridgeway Path

Tumulus

Gallop

Folly Down

83

164

Folly Barn

173

Gore Hill

83

Hodcott Down

Abingdon Lane Down

BS

Sheep Down

Gallop

Berkshire Circular Route

West Ilsley

35

Gallop

Gallop

Gallop

Tumulus

PO

149

Gallop

Mound

EAST ILSLE

82

82

Hodcott House

122

115

Cattle Grid

West Ilsley Stables

Windmill House

147

Cattle Grid

113

Gallop

Berkshire Circular Route

Berkshire Circular Route

81

Woolvers Road (Tk)

Beechtree Hedge Farm

East Ilsley

81

Windmill Down

48

Pit (dis)

Yewtree Hill

Resr

49

Sch

36

Chalk Pit Road

Contours are given in metres
The vertical interval is 5m

77

Shortly beyond the summit of Several Down **37**, yet another gallop leaves the Ridgeway to the south as well as a bridleway, and a little after these another bridleway crosses the Ridgeway, the one to the right being part of the circular route below. The views to the north are delightful. Sparsely scattered lines of trees, like rows of shaving brushes, punctuate the landscape. At the point where the lane from Ilsley Barn Farm merges with the Ridgeway there is another of the welcome drinking water taps with trough for animals and hitching rail for horses by the side of the track. The route also becomes a concrete lane and, about 330 yards further on, a byway crosses it. Another 300 yards or so brings you to another byway which crosses the concrete lane. Do not be tempted to continue straight on along the road. To the right, the byway heads once more into East Ilsley while the road ahead leads to Superity Farm and then to Compton **38**, where there is a research establishment of the Agricultural and Food Research Council's Institute for Animal Health.

A CIRCULAR WALK TO EAST ILSLEY

5½ miles (9 km) (see maps on pages 77 and 79)

Begin at the parking space on the Ridgeway at Bury Down **34** where the minor road from West Ilsley **35** crosses the Ridgeway. Follow the Ridgeway in a south-easterly direction under the A34 trunk road and continue on past the trig point on Several Down. Turn right at the next circular route waymark and follow some gallops into East Ilsley **36**. Where the track meets the road, turn right and continue straight through the village heading roughly east, passing again under the A34. Notice the winding mechanism of the disused village well by the duck pond. Look, too, at the 13th-century Church of St Mary and the Hall and Kennet House. You will come to another waymark directing you towards Windmill Down. About 1¼ miles (2 km) from the A34, turn sharp right and then right again. After about 880 yards the way turns left and passes West Ilsley Stables which are on your right. Follow the metalled road to the eastern outskirts of West Ilsley. Turn right on to a minor road and then soon after fork left on to a route returning you to the Ridgeway. Turn left and return to the car park.

Further details of this walk are in West Berkshire Council's leaflet: *East/West Ilsley Circular Walk.*

The route now turns sharp left heading in a north-easterly direction and returning to partly rutted, partly grassy, partly chalky track – typical Ridgeway. Compton Downs are to your left and, on either side, the rolling downland stretches away into the distance. On reaching the valley bottom, the Ridgeway is lined with trees. There is a bridleway to Compton which is only 1½ miles (2.5 km) from the Ridgeway, regularly used by racehorses for access to gallops. Over a bridge, and the line of a dismantled railway is clearly marked by trees, fences, and the original cutting. From here you can see the Ridgeway snaking up the hillside ahead as a creamy white track, which can be slippery in wet weather. A footpath leads off to the left but your way continues straight on, ascending gently at first but then

Contours are given in metres
The vertical interval is 5m

Compton

more steeply after about 650 yards. Just after the point where a track joins the Ridgeway from the north-west and where there are gallops and a rifle range to the left, the track forks. Take the right fork as the signpost indicates, and head south-east once more. In the area directly to the east of the fork, there is the site of a Roman temple on Lowbury Hill, but you pass south of it and nothing can be seen bar the hill itself.

This is fine downland and, in April, the sheep may be bleating in the fields over which the lapwings wheel and call, while pigeons coo from the isolated copses. Halfway up the next rise, there is a small copse and a criss-crossing of a number of tracks leading to Compton, Lowbury Hill, and the largish village of Blewbury some $2\frac{1}{2}$ miles (4 km) away. After another 550 yards and two-thirds of the way up the next slope, there is another 'crossroads' with tracks going off to right and left, but with the route straight ahead marked Ridgeway. Very shortly after, the path forks again, and the Ridgeway follows the left fork slightly south of east. To the right is the village of Aldworth **39** where the church with its great stone effigies, the 'Aldworth Giants', is well worth a look and where there is an excellent pub, The Bell, but to get there would mean quite a diversion.

Contours are given in
The vertical interval

As I walked along one April, courting yellowhammers were so preoccupied with their own pursuits that they seemed not to be aware of my presence as they flew, beak to tail, ahead of me. After a further quite steep climb of about 33 yards the going eases and begins to level out. From here it is more or less downhill all the way to Streatley; and soon the Goring gap comes into view. This beautiful, comparatively narrow gorge-like cutting in the Thames breaks through the chalk ridge in a north-west to south-east direction. To the right the impressive hollow of Streatley Warren **40** stretches out in a most attractive vista with the green- and straw-coloured slopes dotted with isolated trees and small copses. Do not be tempted to take the track into the woods unless you have time for a walk. There is a delightful gamekeeper's cottage, which sometimes has teas available, just at the entrance to Town Copse and, if you were to continue along that way, you would pass through the very well-kept Well Barn Estate, eventually reaching the A 417 Blewbury Road. Returning to the Ridgeway, continue to the bottom of the steepest part of the descent, close to another Warren Farm. Here the way becomes a metalled lane, and there is car parking space for perhaps a dozen cars.

orth   Contours are given in metres
       The vertical interval is 5m

Continue on down the lane for about 1½ miles (2.5 km) past a charming wooden cottage with its brick-built chimney stack, and Thurle Grange with its newly developed housing. Now Goring and Streatley Golf Course comes into view on the right and a public footpath, in fact marked as the Old Ridgeway, crosses it to join the B4009 road just west of Streatley, but the actual Ridgeway National Trail continues along the road, eventually reaching the A417. Pass the rather grand-looking clubhouse and then, just before reaching the road, there is the entrance on the right to the National Trust property of Lough Down which is open to the public.

Turn right on to the A417 (if you are travelling westwards, the lane from the A417 to the Ridgeway is marked Rectory Road). A little further on, where the road joins the A329, turn right again into the main village of Streatley **41** on the west bank of the River Thames. The two main roads meet at a dangerous corner; it is best to cross to the eastern side of the A417 *before* crossing to the eastern side of the A329. Just before the traffic lights, there is a bus stop where you can catch buses to Oxford or Reading (see page 141 for details of the Ridgeway Public Transport Guide). If you want to stay overnight at the youth hostel, just continue past the traffic lights for some 55 yards; you will find it on the right-hand side of the road.

For those who are staying in Goring **42**, on the other side of the river, or who are continuing along the Ridgeway, turn left at the traffic lights down the hill towards the Thames. Before you reach the river, on the left-hand side of the road, there is an attractive church with a square, flint, perhaps Norman tower. This is the Parish Church of St Mary at Streatley-on-Thames in the diocese of Oxford. The church was built in the 13th century although there was probably a place of worship on the present site in Saxon times and relics of Roman origin have been found in the churchyard. Apart from the tower, the church was rebuilt in 1864 although elements of the older buildings have been retained. On the little road leading to the church, another attractive building is the malthouse.

The official boundary separating Streatley from Goring is just before the first of the two bridges crossing the Thames. On the left is the rather grand, and much extended, Swan Hotel with its moored boats and floating function rooms. This spot is very popular with tourists in summer. There is also the rather curious, red-brick, probably Victorian creation of a village hall with its pagoda-like clock tower. If you are unfamiliar with

Oxfordshire and its breweries, it is well worth sampling Brakspeare's Ales, which are brewed in Henley-on-Thames, in one of the attractive pubs, such as the John Barleycorn or the riverside Old Leatherne Bottle.

The Thames Path, another National Trail, opened in 1996, meets the Ridgeway at Streatley, and continues to Wallingford up the western side of the river.

A sheep fair at East Ilsley c. 1906.

East Ilsley sheep fairs

The village of East Ilsley **36** used to be called 'Market Ilsley' because it was an important centre for sheep sales, being close to the Ridgeway and in a sheep-rearing area. Indeed, the first records of sheep fairs at East Ilsley can be traced to medieval times; then in 1620 Sir Francis Moore, as lord of the manor, received a charter to hold a market for sheep and corn. Once or twice a month on Wednesdays from January to September the village was host to farmers from all over southern England. By the middle of the 18th century some 80,000 sheep could be penned in the village at the annual fairs, which were larger than the Wednesday markets and made the village a hive of industry, supporting 13 public houses, many famed for their ale.

One local resident has clear childhood memories of the pre-First World War fairs and 'the different faces of the sheep; some black, some white and the round chubby faces of the lambs – but all with brown, expressionless eyes, no doubt longing to be away from East Ilsley and back on the downs in peace'. Shepherds would drive the sheep to East Ilsley from as far away as Salisbury, trekking across the downs, and it was really the coming of motorised transport that contributed to the decline of the fairs. The last great sheep fair was held in 1934; attempts to revive them in the 1970s were shortlived, however.

7 Streatley to Mongewell Park

through Goring on Thames, South Stoke and North Stoke
5½ miles (8.8 km)

About 100 yards after you have crossed the second of the two bridges between Streatley **41** and Goring **42**, turn left into Thames Road almost immediately opposite Goring village hall. Continue along this road to a footpath which you follow to another road. Turn left and continue straight ahead. Where the road turns sharply to the right and passes under a railway bridge, your route goes straight ahead.

Here, the Ridgeway is sandwiched between the Thames to the left and the railway line. The path comes out on to a road with the Old Leatherne Bottle public house on your left. Head straight on. You will see a small sailing dinghy park and the boathouse of Goring on Thames Sailing Club on the left. There is a large, red-brick, Victorian property to the right and, at this point, the metalled road becomes a gravelled driveway once again. There are splendid lawns leading down to the river with its weeping willows and pleasure boats. In the trees all around there may, in spring and summer, be the harsh chiffchaff song from which the little brown warbler gets its name, as well as the descending melodic warble of the willow warbler.

As the driveway becomes a narrow dirt path again, it emerges into more open fields between the river and the railway line on the embankment to the right. On the left is a reed bed with an occasional willow leading down to the river which is picked out by a line of taller trees along its bank. On reaching the first houses of South Stoke, go left on to the road and pass another public house, The Perch and Pike, and see ahead the tower of South Stoke Church with its Victorian schoolhouse.

The flint-built, but partly cement-rendered church of St Andrew was built in the 15th century but has been repaired and altered even as recently as the 1960s. In 1974 Oxfordshire Rural Community Council decided that the churchyard was worth an award. Further on, at the road junction, you turn left and head towards the river again. Here you part company with the Swan's Way, a 65-mile (105-km) long bridleway which runs from Goring on Thames to Salcey Forest in Northamptonshire.

The route goes over a little bridge, crossing a small stream, and there are reed beds to the right. At the end of the lane, turn right through a gate and on to the open river bank.

Contours are given in metres
The vertical interval is 5m

Now follow the Thames, which winds roughly northwards, for nearly 2 miles (about 3 km) on soft, springy turf. Note the arches of Moulsford Railway Bridge **44**, built by Isambard Kingdom Brunel (1839), which are dramatically oblique, their brickwork having been ingeniously laid askew.

Half a mile (1 km) after the bridge turn right along a gravel drive towards some houses, turning left again after roughly 20 yards to another narrow dirt footpath, with North Stoke just three-quarters of a mile (just over 1 km) away. As I passed in April there were Canada geese honking out their sentry calls by the river and a green woodpecker yaffled in a nearby tree. Sitting on the ridges of the ploughed field was a pair of reed buntings, and pheasants revealed their presence by klaxon notes.

You come to a small concrete footbridge across a rivulet beyond which there is a gate. Over this, continue across the field to the gate on the other side. The path continues to be obvious with the houses of North Stoke **45** now appearing ahead. The path looks as though it wants to continue around the field but the way actually forks to the left through a gate marked with a yellow arrow. The path here is narrow, lined with trees and with old, rather open woodland between it and the river. There are houses and gardens on the right. After another gate the flint tower of a church is visible and the footpath passes through yet another gate in a brick wall and into the churchyard. The path through the churchyard is obvious and leads to the path from the lych gate at the entrance. Churchyards can frequently provide good wildlife habitats, so it is worth taking a few moments to listen and watch for birds.

Stop and look at the church. It has real charm and a feeling of great antiquity. There was a 7th century Saxon church on this site but even the comparatively 'modern' church which still stands was built in the mid-13th century. Among its many fascinating features are the rather faded wall paintings which date back to the 14th century. Photocopied sheets inside the church will give you more information on its history and architecture.

Leave the churchyard via the main path and the lych gate, but, before you finally depart, notice the sundial which was erected to those who served their country in the First World War. You come out on to a metalled road with Rectory Farmhouse on the left, via the village hall, or was it a church hall or schoolhouse perhaps, which was built in 1864.

Contours are given in metres
The vertical interval is 5m

Continue along the village street past Brick Lodge and the Old Mill on the right. Cross the millstream and, eventually, the road peters out into a driveway. Carry straight on into a broad bridleway between fences and trees with the path hedged on both sides passing through a golf course. Pass through a gateway and follow the bridleway through a field of rough grazing. On the left is a stand of mature poplars which line the approach to Carmel College, until recently a Jewish public school occupying the grounds of Mongewell Park **46**. The school has created a small nature reserve in the wet ground behind the poplars to encourage flowers, insects and birds which flourish in wetland habitats. In spring look out for the bright yellow March marigold and in summer enjoy the song of reed and sedge warblers which visit this area to breed.

When you reach the metalled road, continue straight ahead with a building to your right and a hedge on your left. Ignore all turnings to left and right and after a short while you will pass a lake on your right. During the winter you're likely to see the delightful black and white tufted ducks on this piece of water. Where the road turns right keep straight on, on to a bridleway heralded by a concrete bollard. Follow this paved path until just before it reaches the new Wallingford bypass. The Ridgeway leaves to the right alongside the road and soon enters a narrow strip of woodland, which follows the line of Grim's Ditch (see page 100) intermittently all the way to Nuffield. You have just turned away from the public right of way that could take you to Wallingford **47**, 1¼ miles (2 km) away, if that is your destination.

Wallingford

Today, the busy but attractive Thames-side town of Wallingford **47** takes on a largely Georgian appearance, although recently there has been a little development near the centre and, on the outskirts, there are light industrial sites housing maltings. The history of Wallingford reaches far further back in time than its 18th century demeanour would have visitors believe. It is, in fact, a medieval borough or 'burh'. According to *English Medieval Boroughs – a handlist* by Maurice Berisford and H. P. R. Finberg, Wallingford was first mentioned in a Saxon land grant – as a port – in the year 945. It also has the distinction of a long account in Domesday Book and its castle (the ruins of which are now open to the public) was used as Henry and Matilda's stronghold during the civil war which ended in 1154.

The late 19th century drinking fountain in Wallingford Market Place.

It is worth looking at the bridge over the Thames close by the remains of the castle. Although it was largely rebuilt at the start of the 19th century, parts are medieval and it was certainly in existence at the time of the civil war. The town shows evidence of building in other periods, too, with some fine gabled and timber-framed houses from the 16th and 17th centuries.

The bridge across the Thames at Wallingford dates from medieval times.

8 Mongewell Park to Watlington

via Nuffield and Swyncombe Manor
9½ miles (15.1 km)

This section of the Ridgeway takes you along Grim's Ditch **48** and up into the Chiltern Hills, past Nuffield Common before descending through the scarp valleys to the little town of Watlington, half a mile away from the Trail.

If you are joining the Ridgeway from Wallingford, retrace your steps along the riverside footpath, then go under the bypass and turn left at **A** onto the Ridgeway. You now have to walk close to the new road for a few hundred yards but you then go through a kissing gate in the fence to your right onto a woodland path. You may see wrens fly low over the ground, and hear chiffchaffs sing their repetitive but welcome song. As you approach the road, the grassy track through the trees climbs a little. Go through a gate and out of the trees, cross the road, bearing right and taking care as the traffic is very fast. Pass through a gate and ascend past Lark Rise on to the line of Grim's Ditch **48**.

Contours are given in r
The vertical interval i

Continue to follow the path, walking on top of the bank. The remains of Grim's Ditch are hardly impressive in height here though its length leads one to believe that its construction must have been a major undertaking, even if no one knows what its exact purpose was (see page 100).

Because of the denseness of the shrubbery on either side of the track here, which is a bridleway, only occasional glimpses of the surrounding countryside can be caught, but after the minor road from Crowmarsh Gifford at Cart Gap more of the landscape can be seen.

From Cart Gap, the Trail descends gently to another minor road which follows the line of the old Icknield Way, then the footpath takes you slowly uphill towards Oaken Copse, a marvellous place for bluebells in May. The path of the Ridgeway through the copse is clear enough, and then it descends again before the climb up Bachelor's Hill. Look out for more violets along the way.

From Bachelor's Hill, the bank and ditch are much more in evidence, and here the remains are certainly impressive. You walk through a mixture of trees and open fields up and down hill, past a cottage where a water tap has kindly been provided, until you reach a T-junction. Here you go left (north) and ascend on

urs are given in metres
vertical interval is 5m

a winding track, then onto a headland path before reaching The White House on the edge of the hamlet of Nuffield.

Turn right on to the quiet road. Pass Nuffield parish church **49** on the right with its short, shingle-clad tower; here there is a friendly sign to Ridgeway walkers, offering them water and shelter. May this sign long remain; thank you, Rector! Here you are 700 feet (212 metres) above sea level, the highest point in the southern Chilterns. Consequently, this place was of great importance long before there was a church here. The simple stone font, with its wooden cover, may be Saxon. It is thought that the four walls of the nave were built as long ago as AD 634, although the bulk of the church is made more recent, being about 900 years old.

Look for the Ridgeway sign opposite the church and head across a field and then through a gate onto the Nuffield Common Golf Course **50**. Your way across this busy course is marked by seven numbered white posts with the acorn symbol, each of which can be seen from its neighbour. After crossing two fairways (look carefully first), you go into some trees and the path takes you past Fairway Cottage, seemingly through the front garden, and comes out on to the A423 road which leads to Nettlebed and Wallingford. There is parking for a few cars, a telephone box and bus stop, and, just up the hill, the Crown public house with its quiet but friendly welcome.

From here, you continue down the grass steps and cross the road diagonally to the left, taking great care as visibility is poor and the traffic fast. Enter the small woodland through a kissing gate, aiming to the north-west. After leaving the wood, the path crosses open fields. White posts indicate the way across them, then you go straight through a narrow strip of woodland. Once out of the trees, aim for the white post across the fields, obviously in an uphill direction. Continue in roughly the same direction between lines of thorn trees until you meet a rutted farm track. Continue past Ewelme Park **51** on your left, an impressive mock-Elizabethan house with its neatly mown lawns and rather incongruous, modern-looking windows. Shortly after passing the house, go straight over the crossing track and through the farmyard, bearing right out of it.

Aim for the Plantation where you bear left to the north. This is rich, open farmland punctuated by a number of plantations. Follow the headland path to the strangely named wood of Jacob's Tent, where the path descends quite steeply through delightful, open woodland. Fortunately, waymarking here

Contours are given in metres
The vertical interval is 5m

makes navigation very straightforward and this part of the walk passes through lovely, memorable countryside. At the end of the woods, go through a gate and descend across a field. For me, this area of Swyncombe House **52** is one of the most delightful interludes of the whole of the Ridgeway walk. Here we are, for a brief moment, walking among the epitome of rolling, rich, soft, green, typically English landscape which creates the impression that it has scarcely changed for generations.

On reaching the lane, Ladies Walk, turn right, heading more east of north for a while. After about 440 yards you pass through a gate. To the right is Swyncombe House. Swyncombe Manor was held by the Abbey of Bec in Normandy between 1086 and 1460. The bridleway takes you round to the right, past the beautifully restored little Church of St Botolph's, dating back to the 11th century with 13th and 14th century bells.

Just past the church, the lane bears to the left with the Rectory on your right. A close look at this house reveals that the two large sash windows to the right of the front door, and one above, are false. A short distance on the Ridgeway crosses a quiet minor road and enters a large field through a gate. The hard, chalky path along the left-hand edge of the field now descends quite steeply ahead into another valley before rising again, just as steeply, to enter a mixed wood of mainly conifers and beech. Tree stumps here bear witness to the damage caused by the storms in January 1990. Continue along the path through the woodland to the crest of the hill where there are views to the north-west with Britwell Salome House just visible in the distance.

The path winds down the hill, potentially slippery in places, and as you emerge from Dean Wood at the bottom of the hill the Ridgeway bears north-west. In a further $\frac{1}{2}$ mile the track turns sharply to the right just after passing the buildings of North Farm on the left. You are now on the Icknield Way **53**, which you first crossed part-way along Grim's Ditch (the Swan's Way rejoins from the left). After about 440 yards cross the minor road leading from Britwell Salome and continue in a north-easterly direction, eventually reaching Lys Farm House where the path continues in the same direction but, this time, as a metalled road. Cross Howe Road (the B480) near Icknield House and continue along the track with Watlington Hill to the north-east. Keep on until you reach the crossing with Hill Road which leads down into the small town of Watlington **54** and to a pleasant camp site at White Mark Farm.

Contours are given in metres
The vertical interval is 5m

Trees overshadow the path along Grim's Ditch, an ancient earthwork with a possible defensive significance.

Grim's Ditch

Grim is another name for the Nordic god Odin, and the term 'Grim's Ditch' **48** was used by the Anglo Saxons for various linear earthworks, probably as a means of explaining the origins of the feature of which they had little understanding. Who constructed these earthworks and for what purpose is unknown, not least in the absence of contemporary literary sources or detailed archaeological investigation which might establish dating evidence or identify associated archaeological features. It is possible that these earthworks formed some type of defensive network associated with some of the nearby Ridgeway hill forts and are therefore prehistoric in date. However, given that the hill forts are not all contemporary and may not have been within the same tribal control, this is hard to establish.

Another explanation is that the ditch may have been a type of boundary: it could have been used either on a local basis as a stock boundary, or on a wider scale to denote tribal boundaries.

Ewelme

The straggling village of Ewelme, nestling in the Chiltern foothills, is only 2½ miles (4 km) from either Ewelme Park or Swyncombe House, and is well worth a visit. It is best known for its splendid group of 15th century buildings – church, school and almshouses – and for its associations with Chaucer's granddaughter, Alice, Duchess of Suffolk (look out for 'Dame Alice Farm' further along the Ridgeway national trail near Watlington).

The Perpendicular church of St Mary the Virgin is high on the hill above the village. It is well preserved – the local Parliamentary commander protected it from destruction during the Civil War – and has interesting furnishings, brasses and two magnificent tombs: that of Duchess Alice herself, as well as the tomb of her father, Thomas Chaucer. It is also where Jerome K. Jerome, author of *Three Men in a Boat*, is buried. The almshouses, founded in 1437 by the Suffolks, are built around a small courtyard at the west end of the church, and are still in use today.

The name Ewelme is derived from 'lawelme' – a spring source – and even today the spring feeds the cress-filled chalk stream running beside the main street through the village. Pleasant cottages and a quiet location help to make Ewelme one of the prettiest villages in the Chilterns.

The 15th century almshouses at Ewelme, which enclose a small courtyard.

9 Watlington to Princes Risborough

past Lewknor and Chinnor
11 miles (17.5 km)

Much of the Ridgeway in this stretch is on the Upper Icknield Way (see page 110), which followed the lower chalk shelf at the foot of the north-western scarp of the Chilterns. The route is all on byways, RUPPs, bridleways or country lanes, so this is a section that is suitable for horseriders or cyclists.

If you have stayed in Watlington 54, then to rejoin the route just walk back up Hill Road and turn left, below Watlington Hill, on to the Ridgeway. As you walk, look ahead and to the right for the triangular-shaped Watlington White Mark above the Ridgeway. At this point there is parking space for a few cars.

The lower parts of the hills are wood-cladded and, to the left, the flat farmland stretches out across the Oxfordshire plain. In some hawthorn bushes to my left, I had marsh tits for company on my April walk. After about 550 yards the track narrows and plunges between lines of trees and in another 200 yards it crosses the metalled lane which is the Oxfordshire Way, a 65-mile (105-km) recreational route from Bourton-on-the-Water in the Cotswolds to Henley-on-Thames.

The Trail continues through the trees and is obviously used by horseriders. The shallow bank on the right-hand side of the path was pockmarked with what could have been rabbit burrows although, at the entrance to one, there were the remains of a bird, which might have been the leftovers from a fox's meal, suggesting a change of ownership for at least one of the holes. I heard chiffchaffs and the occasional pheasant, and saw robins, finches, dunnock, tits and wrens. A rabbit, scutt showing white, dashed across the lane in front of me. There were clusters of white and purple violets at the edges of the track.

Slowly the Ridgeway begins to ascend with the steep, tree-clad, tumulus-like mound of Shirburn Hill to the right. In the distance, there is a barely audible hum which gradually increases. A glance at the map shows that the M40 motorway is at least $1\frac{1}{2}$ miles (2.5 km) away but, even at this distance, it makes its noisy presence felt. The green lane continues to be fringed with ancient beeches, younger willows and occasional elms and yews, as well as dead trees. Emerging from the trees,

the track becomes broad and grassy once more, rising slowly uphill towards the motorway, which is now clearly visible on the immediate horizon directly ahead, as well as cutting a broad, grey swathe across the countryside to the left. To the right rises Bald Hill where there is part of a National Nature Reserve and, beyond the motorway, Beacon Hill, with the other part of the reserve. As the traffic roar grew louder, I realised why the siting of this road caused such controversy – in this case, the planners had their way and the National Nature Reserve of Aston Rowant 55 was cut in two.

Just before reaching the M40, the Ridgeway crosses a metalled road running between Hill Farm and Lewknor, a little more than half a mile (1 km) to the north-west. On the other side of the tunnel under the M40, the track is broad and scored by ruts in places but, by walking on the grassy verges or on the ridge in the middle, the going can be quite comfortable. Leaving the noise of the motorway behind, Beacon Hill rises up to the right. Now the track follows a tree-lined bank. The National Nature Reserve of Aston Rowant, part owned, part leased, and part held by agreement, occupies 315 acres (126 hectares) and includes chalk grassland with several kinds of orchid, and scrub on the slopes where juniper, privet and yew grow in abundance. There is beech woodland, too, with ash, wild cherry and oak. Further information about the reserve can be obtained from English Nature's regional office at Foxhold House, Crookham Common, Newbury, or from the Warden at 1 Field Farm Cottages, Menmarsh Road, Worminghall, Aylesbury, Bucks.

The A40 road, which you cross next, can be busy although, of course, the M40 now takes most of the traffic which once used this major arterial road from London. The brick and flint house here, Beacon Cottage Country Guest House, helpfully hangs a dustbin bag on its boundary fence along the Ridgeway.

The tree-root-bound rough track continues straight ahead with primroses brightening the way in spring. The tree-covered ridge of Aston Hill is to the right and, again, the going could be muddy in wet weather. In April, the fields to the right were sown with perfectly uniform green grass and oilseed rape. Ahead and to the right, the wooded slopes of Kingston Hill rise to its trig point at 678 feet (206 metres) and are probably best viewed in late October when the autumn colours are at their best. This is another stretch of the route which may be improved in coming years. You now cross a bridleway which leads to Aston Rowant to the north and Aston Hill to the south. In this area, for the first time along the Ridgeway, I saw the charming little long-tailed tits flitting among the trees. Ahead, and a little to the right, the white marker posts of a point-to-point racecourse, used only three or four times a year, come into view. The going here can still be wet and rutted in parts. Cross a track leading to Grove Farm and the way becomes grassy again.

Soon you cross the minor road which leads to Kingston Blount **56** in the north. The route continues straight ahead as a

Contours are given in metres
The vertical interval is 5m

Contours are given in metres
The vertical interval is 5m

broad, grassy, hedge-lined track. Ahead and a little to the left rise the twin chimneys of the Chinnor cement works, now closed; the future of the site is still uncertain. And immediately to the left of the path, the line of a railway, which is in use only from the cement works eastwards, is picked out by its hedges. Beside the cement works are water-filled quarry pits, one of which has been made into a nature reserve attracting Canada geese. The path ascends with Oakley Hill to the right before dropping down to the road from Crowell Hill to Chinnor **57**, half a mile away.

Across the road the track is creamy white and chalky once again and climbs gradually along the lower slopes of Bledlow Ridge **58**, on the edge of the woods. Look out for dog's mercury and primroses. At Wain Hill Cottage, turn right by a red-brick

urs are given in metres
vertical interval is 5m

house, and once again you seem to be intruding into a garden but there are signposts to reassure you. You are now walking eastwards and have crossed into Buckinghamshire.

With the scarp of the Bledlow Ridge rising steeply ahead and to the right, this is an attractive spot. Once again the trail begins gently to rise as a broad lane on the edge of the wood. Emerging from the trees, and travelling a little to the south of east, tracks lead off to left and right. Continue onwards to where you see the Ridgeway signpost, at which point you leave the Icknield Way, through a gate to the right, and go into a field which you cross diagonally. On the far, upward slope of the field to the right of some trees, the path can be seen working its way up across the hill in a direction a little south of east. At the top of the slope, the rise of Lodge Hill can be seen.

The path stays close to the fence, goes through a gate and carries on down with the fence on your right to the Bledlow road, where you go through another gate on to the road, which you cross diagonally to the left to the next gate. The path is then quite obvious across the field. After another gate the broad path across the next field is clearly defined forking to the left. Lodge Hill seems to grow ever closer. You are now heading towards a line of coppiced trees. Go through the gate, after which you turn immediately to the right. Follow the path along the edge of the field with the trees on your right until the boundary of the field turns sharply left. The Ridgeway route continues ahead and upwards on to the slopes of Lodge Hill.

As it rises to the summit of the hill the path becomes quite steep. This is soft, rabbit-grazed turf with small hazel trees and wild roses. On the long, high ridge, the views to both sides are splendid. Continue across the hill towards a line of trees and through a gate before descending. In fact, you must bear a little left down the hill but do not wander right, into a danger area where there may be shooting. Lodge Hill would make a lovely spot for a summer picnic.

Continue downhill through a couple of gates towards a gap in a hedge which meets the one you are following. Go through the gap, and follow the acorn and blue arrow to the left of a well-clipped hawthorn hedge. Follow the hedge downhill and, 100 yards before the electricity pylons, turn left. Follow the path, keeping the hedge on your right, as it winds down towards the minor road which leads to Saunderton, about 1¼ miles (2 km) to the north. From here it is possible to see Lacey Green **59** on the hillside ahead with its restored smock mill, one of the oldest in Britain.

Cross the road on to the gravel drive – which is a footpath – that leads to a single red-brick house. Go to the right of the house and then across the broad field ahead towards a line of trees. At a gate, turn right and follow a hedge with a golf course to left and right. Bear right, still following the hedge, until you reach another gate and cross the railway line with care. Go through the blackthorn thicket to a kissing gate and then into the field.

Carry on up a slight gradient, keeping the trees in the field just to your left, to another gate. Go through this, over the top of the railway tunnel to a further kissing gate, and then continue straight across the field. Pass directly between two pylons towards two converging hedgerows. The path emerges on to a minor road – the Upper Icknield Way again. (If walking east to west, you need to cross the field at approximately 45°, making for the kissing gate.) Follow the road to the right, and descend to cross Shootacre Lane. On the hillside ahead, you can make out the outline of Whiteleaf Cross carved into the slope, although from here it looks like a white horse. Continue along the road to the A4010 High Wycombe–Princes Risborough road, and turn left towards Princes Risborough **60**. There is a pavement along the right-hand side of the road and, after the quiet of the hills, the traffic noise seems wearing. Just after Culverton Lane, about half a mile on, there is a public footpath to the right which, although it is not the official route, does rejoin it and cut off a corner, provided you do not mind negotiating two stiles.

Contours are given in metres
The vertical interval is 5m

4 km or 2½ miles
A4010 Bradenham

Kissing gate and sign marking the Ridgeway near Princes Risborough.

The official route, as signposted, turns right off the Wycombe Road in about another 100 yards into a cul-de-sac lane called the Upper Icknield Way. The Ridgeway goes north-eastwards, staying on the southern outskirts of the town. You soon pass the point where the short cut mentioned earlier rejoins the route and, a little beyond that, another footpath crosses the way. Soon you pass a school on the left and then some small bungalows, and descend to Brimmers Road. Turn left and walk down to Princes Risborough if you are planning to stop here.

The Icknield Way

The Icknield Way was a trading route from Norfolk to the southwest, which has now largely been absorbed into the present network of roads. Look carefully on the maps; you can follow much of the line of the Icknield Way from the Thames (Streatley was thought to be a major ford) to Ivinghoe, on B roads and tracks, along both the Upper and Lower Ways.

There are many theories as to its history, but it is not as old as the Ridgeway. The name 'Icknield' may derive from the Iceni, who could have used it as a warpath, or from old British words for 'upper'. The fact is that its precise origins are lost in the mists of time. What *is* sure is that it followed ridges, where possible, and the lower chalk shelf, which offered a better route than the 'clay-with-flints' and the thick woodland of the Chilterns. This is the line followed by the Upper Icknield Way; the Lower Way is on the clay and may have been a later, possibly Roman, route.

From Ivinghoe the Icknield Way goes on to Thetford, where it connects with the Peddars Way. The route of the Icknield Way from Streatley to the west is via Blewbury and Wantage to Wanborough, following a line to the north of the Ridgeway. One of the best books on the Icknield Way is Edward Thomas's account of his walk along the way before the First World War; even today much of the landscape he admired is still there to be enjoyed.

10 Princes Risborough to Wendover

past Whiteleaf Cross and Chequers
6 miles (9.5 km)

From Princes Risborough **60**, walk up Brimmers Road to rejoin the Ridgeway on the left, where it follows the Upper Icknield Way. Walk past the backs of houses and turn right, leaving the Icknield Way, opposite the playing fields.

Head uphill towards Risborough Cop and Kop Hill passing a line of thorn trees on the left. Carry straight on and once in the woodland continue up the stepped path soon crossing a footpath. It is steep going here. Before reaching the top of the hill, pass through a gate into a field and bear slightly left between the clumps of hawthorn. Continue uphill heading towards the right edge of the wood ahead. Soon you reach a minor road leading from Brimmers Road. Don't cross the stile on to the road; instead bear sharp left between the woodland and the old hedgeline keeping the wire fence in front of the wood on your right. Go through the gate in the corner and carry on until you come down on to another road. Turn right and then left after 20 yards. The car park for Whiteleaf Cross provided by Buckinghamshire County Council is immediately on your right.

The trees on Whiteleaf Hill were devastated by the 1990 storms but since then many young trees have been replanted. Follow the signs bearing right along a clearly identified path until you emerge on to a grassy clearing with a stone age long barrow on your left. There are splendid views ahead. On the slope of the hill is the Whiteleaf Cross. It is the earliest of the Chiltern hill figures. First documented in 1742, the cross may have been carved by monks in the 15th or 16th centuries for devotional or perhaps navigational purposes.

After a gate you turn right from the clearing into the heart of Giles Wood. Soon passing through another gate you follow the path towards Lower Cadsden with the tree-clad hollow of The Hangings on your right. After a few minutes the way begins to descend sharply to the Cadsdean Road – this can be very slippery in wet weather. On either side of the track the hill plunges away as you walk through the beech woodland. Towards the foot of the hill, go through the kissing gate and bear right into a car park. Parking here is only for the patrons of The Plough public house.

Contours are given in metres
The vertical interval is 5m

Continue past the pub on the left. As you emerge on to the Cadsdean Road, there are two possible routes. The definitive (i.e. 'official') path involves a walk of about 200 yards down the road to the left and then a steep climb northwards, helped by steps, between fences. A far better alternative route involves crossing the Cadsdean Road diagonally towards a post saying 'No horses'.

Go right through the chicane onto a woodland permissive footpath, muddy at times. After 150m go through the kissing gate into the nature reserve, carry on ahead for 10m, then bear left. Follow this narrow path for almost 100m and fork right onto a permissive bridleway. This nature reserve of Grangelands and Pulpit Hill **62** is owned by Bucks County Council and the National Trust but the local naturalists' trust, BBONT, manages it. Here, though, the downland turf has been worn away to the detriment of the landscape and animal life. Riders should use only the marked track and not gallop.

Some distance up the hill, and through another gateway, you cross a bridleway, where the official path joins from the left. Carry on straight ahead and immediately through a kissing gate. With the wooded heights of Pulpit Hill to the right, continue north-eastwards across its lower ridge. Pass the Butts on your right and go into woodland over a stile or through the kissing gate to the left, climbing steps to emerge into a deep cutting (meeting the North Bucks Way).

Turn right and, a little way up the gully, go through the gate on the left. The tumulus on the small hill on your left is Chequers Knap, and you are now in Chequers nature reserve. This reserve supports a galaxy of chalkland plants such as common rock-rose, wild thyme and squinancywort. The valley, or coombe, to the left is one of only three truly native box sites in Britain.

(*Westbound* travellers should look out for the start of the alternative route at the crossing bridleway. The official route goes to the right, and after a few yards turns left through scrub and straight across an arable field to the top of the steep bank, which the path descends to the Cadsdean Road. The alternative route goes straight over the bridleway, across the Grangelands reserve to the Cadsdean Road, emerging almost opposite the road to 'The Plough'.)

Now head slightly north of east across the valley, following a fairly obvious path through curious, undulating, gullied country. At the fence the footpath takes you on to an obvious

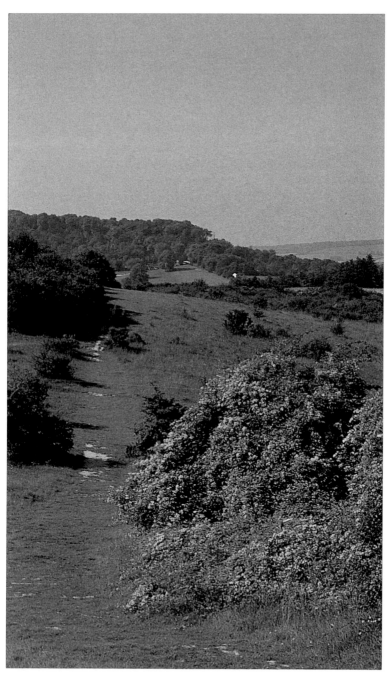

Grangelands and Pulpit Hill, a nature reserve known for its chalk grassland flora.

track and the route bears to the right following the fenceline.

Go through the gate and cross the field for 300 yards; here the path is quite well worn. Aim for the gates on the other side. The path now veers to the south; skirting the northeastern side of Maple Wood to avoid entering the actual grounds of Chequers **64**, the Prime Minister's country residence. This is pleasant, open farmland with the 16th century house of Chequers partly visible behind some trees as you pass a redundant stile and walk by the edge of the wood. At the end of Maple Wood, you are directed across the farmland to the left, through two gates, and on to the drive of Chequers itself. This house was given as a country home for the Prime Minister in 1917 by Lord Lee of Fareham. Cross the gravel drive and head for another gate on the opposite side of the field. Go through this too, cross the road, and follow the broad track into the trees to the left of a group of white houses.

Proceed uphill into the woods following the acorn symbols. This is a fine beech wood, probably looking its best in spring with its new leaves or in its autumn colours. When you reach the shoulder of the hill, turn left and, after about 20 yards, turn right again and into the heart of the wood. Here you must just keep your eyes open to follow the acorns for there is no very obvious path. In parts, however, the way can be rutted by horses' hoofs and quite muddy. In May, bluebells carpet the woodland floor. When you reach a post and rail fence on your right, go over the stile and head left. Turn left over the next stile and then right immediately through the gate on to a minor road heading gently uphill. Almost opposite a red-brick house, a signpost and acorns tell you to cross the road and enter the woodland on Lodge Hill. Once again, follow the acorns through the wood and at the fence go through the kissing gate. Turn left and then bear right towards the edge of the hill. To the left, there are lovely views towards Beacon Hill, and down into the village of Ellesborough, with the church and Ellesborough Manor clearly visible across the golf course.

Once again, you are on a broad swathe of the rabbit-cropped grass which makes comfortable walking. By the trig point at 845 feet (257 metres) atop Coombe Hill **65** there is a grand-looking monument capped with a golden fluted ball to the men of Buckinghamshire who died in the Boer War in South Africa at the turn of the century. The views in all directions are spectacular so, perhaps not surprisingly, this land is in the ownership of the National Trust.

From the monument, simply bear slightly right, taking the lower path towards a hedgeline. The path is obvious and skirts along the edge of the hill until you reach a fenceline. Here, pass through the kissing gate, down a few steps and over the bridleway in the tree-lined gully. This path can be muddy to cross at wet times of the year, but steps have also thoughtfully been provided at the other side to help walkers negotiate the slippery bank. Ahead and to the left, the small town of Wendover comes into view. As you enter the wood, the path descends gradually across Bacombe Hill **66**. Just before what looks like the end of the Bacombe Hill ridge, the path forks to the left down the hill as a broadly defined path on a bank. Even though the road and Wendover are so close, this is pleasant walking. Here, the steepening gradient is eased by broad steps

Contours are given in metres
The vertical interval is 5m

cut into the path. Bacombe Hill is owned and maintained by Buckinghamshire County Council, who are working to re-establish areas of chalk grassland and scrub here, and re-introducing traditional hazel coppice management in the wood-land to the left.

On reaching the B4010, where there is parking for perhaps two cars, turn right and take the road down into Wendover **67**, substantially quieter now since the bypass opened. Cross the bypass and the railway line via the road bridge where Wend-over station is signposted to the left. At a mini-roundabout, continue straight ahead towards Aylesbury and Tring.

The Chiltern beechwoods

Anyone travelling the eastern 'half' of the Ridgeway cannot fail to notice two important natural and not-quite-so-natural fea-tures of the landscape – the chalk escarpment and plateau which comprise the Chiltern Hills and the extensive beechwoods which shade much of that ridge. Deposited in warm Upper Cre-taceous seas some 80 million years ago, the major structures of the chalk rock of south-east England, such as the Chiltern Hills, were formed during the same great heavings of the planet that threw up the Alpine mountain chain about 50 million years later. But it was not until the extensive oakwoods, which once clothed much of England, began to be cleared in Neolithic times that the beech could predominate, even though it is a native English tree. In strict ecological terms, then, beechwoods are not natural, but that hardly matters to passers-through – they seem natural enough now although, in places, evidence of cop-picing does suggest that they have at least been managed. Indeed, they continue to be so in some areas.

The nature of beechwoods is quite different from that of other deciduous woodland, and this becomes obvious as you pass between the tall, smooth, pewter-grey trunks and beneath the dense canopy of light-green leaves up to 100 feet (30 metres) above your head. Even in the brightest days of summer, only a leaf-filtered twilight penetrates to the woodland floor. Apart from the harsh notes of chiffchaffs, the descending, musical trill of willow warblers from high overhead, or the alarm call of a disturbed blackbird, beechwoods are often eerily quiet.

The soils on the Chilterns may vary from deep, rich loams to shallow, acidic types on the clay-with-flints which caps the chalk in places, or, where it does not, thin chalky soil predominates. There are beechwoods to be found on all these

Contours are given in metres
The vertical interval is 5m

6 km or 3½ miles
A413 Great Missenden

soils, although the trees may grow taller where the substrate is richer and deeper. It is the peculiarly shallow and very wide-reaching root system of the beech which enables it to flourish where other trees cannot. And, once it has become established, a beechwood's dense canopy of leaves high above restricts the light so much that few other plants can survive in the darker parts. Thus, in many places, the only other bushes or shrubs to be seen are occasional hollies or yews, although brambles may straggle across quite large areas. At ground level, dog's mercury or sanicle may grow, bird's-nest orchids may throw up their rusty brown flower spikes, often unseen, where the soil is rich in humus from the decaying leaves and lime from the chalk, and, in autumn, there is a variety of fungi associated with the beech trees. Rarely do plants carpet the beechwood floor as they may do in other woodland types.

It is probably safe to say that all of today's Chiltern beech trees have been planted. From about the 17th century, beech wood has had a commercial worth, initially to supply a cheap source of fuel and charcoal for London and then, particularly in the 18th century, for furniture-making, with an industry centred on High Wycombe. In today's slang, 'bodger' is a word often applied to someone who turns out poor-quality work, especially carpentry or DIY. In the 1700s, however, and even in its strictly correct meaning now, a bodger was a craftsman skilled at turning and carving wood, especially beech, to make chairs, and individual bodgers flourished throughout the Chiltern woods. It is likely that the modern slang usage has evolved through an alteration of the word 'botcher' and because a bodger was someone associated with working in wood.

There are few bodgers left today but beechwood is still used for furniture-making, and the Chiltern beechwoods continue to have commercial and leisure-time value.

A CIRCULAR WALK ON THE RIDGEWAY AND NORTH BUCKS WAY

6 miles (10 km) (see maps on pages 113 and 117)

A leaflet describing this route, *The Ellesborough/Kimble Circular Walk*, can be obtained by sending an s.a.e. to Buckinghamshire County Council, Environmental Services Department, County Hall, Aylesbury, Bucks HP20 1UY. The easiest starting point is the railway station and car park to the south of Little Kimble (see map on page 113). From here, walk northwards into Little Kimble on the A4010 Aylesbury road. Then turn right on to a route leading to Ellesborough Manor. From here (see map on page 117), head south and then south-east towards Coombe Hill Farm. Turn right on to the minor road and, shortly afterwards, left then right, following the route marked on the map, eventually climbing up to join the Ridgeway. Follow the Ridgeway briefly south and then west, skirting Chequers **64**, until it joins with the North Bucks Way at Chequers Knap (page 113). Continue north-westwards until you reach the minor road near New Farm. Turn left on to the road but where the North Bucks Way forks off left, continue on the road turning right. Where the road takes a sharp turn to the left, turn right on to a path leading to the B4009 Grove Lane. Turn left, go under the railway, and turn immediately right and back to the station and car park.

Woods are an important part of the Chilterns landscape, but they do need to be managed.

11 Wendover to Wigginton

through Barn Wood and Pavis Wood
6 miles (9.8 km)

A feature of this stretch of the path is the woodlands, some of which are worth taking a side trip to visit; see page 126.

In Wendover **67**, go past the library, toilets and car park on the right. Just before you reach the clock tower and another mini-roundabout turn right towards St Mary's Church and into a narrow lane called Heron Path, as indicated by the Ridgeway signpost. Where a path joins from the right the Ridgeway bears a little to the left with open ground on either side. It soon reaches a stream on the left which it follows for a short distance. After 80 yards or so the Ridgeway crosses a path and after another 80 yards bears right leaving the stream. It now heads upslope towards the church with a pond on the right.

As you reach the road, turn left immediately in front of the church. The churchyard of St Mary the Virgin is well kept, with flowers gracing the flint walls. Follow the minor road past the church to a more major road, cross it and continue straight ahead into a 'no through road', passing to the left of a cream-painted house. You are now heading south-east on the metalled lane towards a line of wooded hills. Past some farm buildings the lane becomes a gravel and dirt track and soon passes a path to the left.

The way ascends towards a red-brick farmhouse with its barn behind – Boswells Farm. Atop the main house, there is a small bell and clock tower with a charming fox weather vane. Continue straight on past a curious little wooden cottage and into a band of woodland where blue periwinkles line the verges. This area is heavily wooded, with much of it under the management of the Forestry Commission.

Carry on towards the hill ahead, passing an entrance to the left. Ignore a fork to the right and after 20 yards or so turn left keeping a wooden gate post on your right. Bear left at yet another fork where there is a wire fence to the right and a small plantation of young conifers. In another 100 yards there is one more fork where, this time, you head right up the hill as indicated, into the open woodland and coppice of Barn Wood, with dog's mercury and occasional clumps of primroses in early spring. Continue up into the wood. When the trees are not in leaf, there are glimpses of the wooded hills and vales to the left.

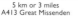

5 km or 3 miles   Contours are given in metres
A413 Great Missenden   The vertical interval is 5m

As the slope eases, the track continues straight on upwards towards a clearing but a yellow arrow indicates that you turn left. The route is easy to follow, and continues to skirt around the edge of the hill; for compass users in a north-easterly direction. Every now and then there are odd hollows by the side of the path. The going here can be muddy especially in wet weather. Eventually the way becomes broad and grassy as you walk among the willow, hazel, hawthorn and beech trees. You are passing through the southern fringes of Wendover Woods, part of the Forestry Commission's Chiltern Forest (see page 126).

Contours are given in metres
The vertical interval is 5m

The track becomes broader as you pass through Hale Wood and occasionally there are paths crossing it. Shortly before Milesfield, pass through a gate and on to a road. Turn right and then immediately left. Descend a little through the mature woodland. To the right is the broad, grassy clearing of Milesfield itself while on the left is the deep wooded vale of The Hale. At the bottom of the slope, turn right at the bottom of the steps up a deep gully where you join a bridleway.

The path bears right after 300 yards, and after passing a cottage on the right you reach Aston Hill Road. Directly

Contours are given in metres
The vertical interval is 5m

opposite, adjacent to a dormer-windowed bungalow, go through a gate in the hedge. After passing the corner of the hedge, aim for the radio mast ahead, keeping the hedge to the right. Just at the end of a small group of conifers, another gate takes you through a wooden fence, where you go diagonally across the field towards the mast and some farm buildings. The compass bearing is 44°. You go through a gate and arrive at the road to the right of the mast. Turn left down the road for a very short distance and then turn right into the wood as indicated. Follow the line of the woods, staying just inside their edge.

Emerging from Pavis Wood on to a minor road take the road almost opposite, which leads towards Hastoe. Your way takes you straight across into Church Lane, as indicated by the Ridgeway sign. Shortly after Marlin Hill Farm, you arrive at Hastoe Cross. It is likely the Ridgeway will soon be diverted here to go through Tring Park. It will be well signed. In the meantime cross the road, pass through a gateway, and go on to a farm track where Wick Wood soon comes into sight.

In about 880 yards you pass the buildings of Wick Farm and the going becomes a neat, hedge-lined, gravel drive. For those stopping in Wigginton, it is possible to carry on past the point where the Ridgeway goes to the left and on to a metalled road with houses on the left. It then joins another road with Wigginton Bottom to the right and Wigginton itself to the left. Another public right of way leads off the minor road into Wigginton **68**.

You could then walk to Tring through Bulls Wood and Tring Park, or take a bus to Tring or Chesham. Alternatively, Tring station is not far along the Ridgeway (see next chapter for directions).

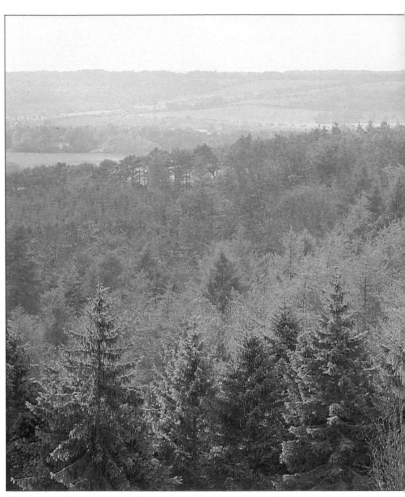

Wendover Woods, where the Forestry Commission offers walks and picnic area

Woods in the area

You may want to take time to divert from the Ridgeway to explore one of the woods in this part of the Chilterns.

Wendover Woods **69**, owned by the Forestry Commission, cover 400 acres (160 hectares) and offer a variety of walks, picnic areas, a wayfaring course and trails for horseriders (for which a permit is required). As well as broadleaf woods, there is mixed woodland at Aston Hill Coppice and beech hangers. Contact the Forestry Commission's Chilterns office for details: tel. Wendover (01296) 625825.

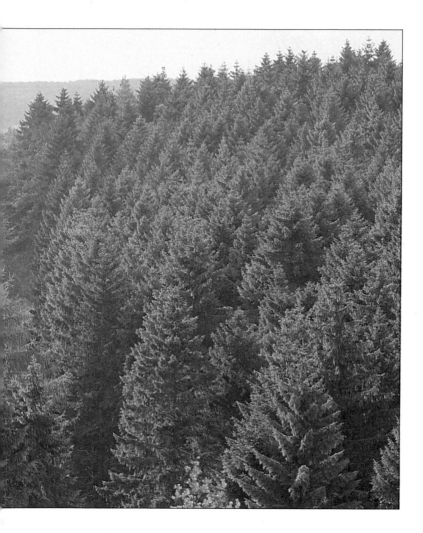

At the north-eastern end of Wendover Woods is the 70-acre (28-hectare) BBONT reserve, Dancer's End **70**, with its more typical Chiltern woodland. This reserve is best in spring and summer, when a rich variety of plant species can be seen.

On a much larger scale is the Ashridge Estate **71**, to the south-east of Ivinghoe Beacon. This 4,000-acre (1,600-hectare) National Trust property has been famous for its beeches and oaks since the 18th century and has many paths which lead through the woods and heaths. Access is via the B4506 between Ringshall and Berkhamsted, or from the Ridgeway via a number of footpaths and bridleways from Tring station onwards.

12 Wigginton to Ivinghoe Beacon

past Tring Station and Pitstone Hill
5½ *miles* *(8.8 km)*

At last, the final stretch of your journey along the Ridgeway. This part of the path takes you down from the woodland and on to the chalk grassland of the Ivinghoe Hills. Since the path passes by Tring station, it is a very accessible section of the Ridgeway.

Before reaching the end of the gravel drive and the road to Wigginton **68**, turn left over a stile as indicated by a Ridgeway signpost. You are now on a grassy footpath, with the backs of houses to the right and a fence and fields to the left, heading for Bull's Wood. Just before reaching the wood, turn sharp right and climb over a stile. Here a Ridgeway sign points the way and, at another, the path soon makes a left turn past some houses in a direction a little west of north. Cross a lane and there is now a laurel hedge on the right and another plantation on the left. Ignore any turnings into the wood. Quite a lot of this woodland has now been replanted with young trees interspersed with bushes of broom. Beside a brick house with mock Tudor chimneys there is a stile, and the Ridgeway turns to the right to take you out on to a minor road.

Cross the road, go through a gate, and take time to admire the attractive views to the left across the plain and to the hills ahead. You are now travelling along a fence-lined path towards Langton Wood. You pass a trig point on the path. Somewhat surprisingly, for there is no real feeling of great elevation, you are at a height of 710 feet (216 metres). To the left, the roar of traffic on the downslope side is from the A41(M). From here to the next road, keeping the wood to your left, you have to negotiate another seven kissing gates, all needed to take you through the small fields. When you reach the minor road, turn right and shortly left.

Carry on down, crossing the hedgeline after a few hundred yards, and then over the A41(M) using the footbridge. When you reach the A41, which follows the line of the Roman road, Akeman Street, cross it and walk down the verge to the right. At Pen Beech Lodge go through the gate next to it and follow the path towards Tring station. This might once have been a pleasant path with the beech hedge and the woodland to the

Chalk Pit
Chalk Pit
Folly Farm
Folly Bridge
Pit (dis)
14
Wks
Bulbourne Farm
Park Hill Farm
Marsh Croft Farm
Towing Path
13
Marshcroft Cottages
Marshcroft Lane
Towing Path
Clarke's Spring
Northfield Grange
Pitstone Hill **75**
74
Goldi Spri
Pit (dis)
Ridgeway
Aldbury Nowers
Tumulus
Tumulus
Pit (dis)
Grim's Ditch
Westland Farm
Ridgeway
71 →
Tring Station **73**
Hotel
ALD
Ashridge Estate
12
Station Road
Cow Lane Farm
Pendley Farm
Pendley Manor
Chestnut Wood
Pendley Beeches
Lodge Bushes
Tring ← **72**
ley Farm
A 4251
ndon Road
ROMAN RD
Meridian Street
A 41(T)
New Ground Farm
Towing Path
11
Ridgeway
The Twist
216
Langton Wood
Pit (dis)
New Ground
Bottom House Lane
Park Farm
Hemp Lane
Wigginton
223 **68**
Ridgeway
Wood
Sch
Pit
Hill Green Farm
Cow Roast
94
95
Berkhamstead
3 km or 2 miles

Contours are given in metres
The vertical interval is 5m

129

left but it is now marred by a tall wire fence supported on strong wooden posts. After the next gate you reach a gravel drive and you are still heading downslope. Do not be tempted to turn right here. Where the drive turns left into the wood continue onwards on the grassy path – this is the obvious direction.

There is a kissing gate on to a minor road. Turn left. In about 275 yards you will reach a T-junction. To the left is the main part of the town of Tring **72**, about 1½ miles (2.5 km) along Station Road. Turn right, however, and cross the Grand Union Canal. In another 275 yards there is the Royal Hotel, offering cream teas and hotel and restaurant facilities as well as bars open to non-residents. There is a bus stop opposite. Shortly after this, there is Tring railway station **73** which, therefore, is some distance from the town centre. Cross the railway line and continue along the road past the minor road to the left. Continue along the main road, then turn left on to a metalled driveway which heads uphill and is clearly signposted. There is a wooden gate here. Continue straight on leaving the hard track to head towards the fence. Pass through another gate and turn sharp left. Continue gently uphill on the tree-lined path passing Westland Farm on the left. This is a bridleway. Although it scarcely shows on the map you are following some quite old-looking woodland to the left of the track. At a crossing of paths, fork right on to a broad track heading uphill through Duchie's Piece nature reserve, managed by the Hertfordshire and Middlesex Naturalist Trust, and into some woodland. Where the track comes into a gully with the remains of a section of another Grim's Ditch visible to the right, turn to the left and up steps. The route undulates around the edge of the hill following the lines of Grim's Ditch **74**. It is pleasant walking through the wood; it continues to be waymarked and any rises are aided by the steps.

As I walked along in April, I was accompanied by the eerie yowling of peacocks, which I guessed must have been at Northfield Grange on the low ground to the west, and I was also aware of the presence of marsh tits. The way is now a broad, undulating dirt path through the woodland and cannot be mistaken. The route then begins to descend again across Pitstone Hill **75** and the redundant cement works seem to fill the whole of the view ahead – a real blot on the landscape. If you are able to forget it, however, the patchwork of fields and buildings in the valley offers a more pleasing aspect.

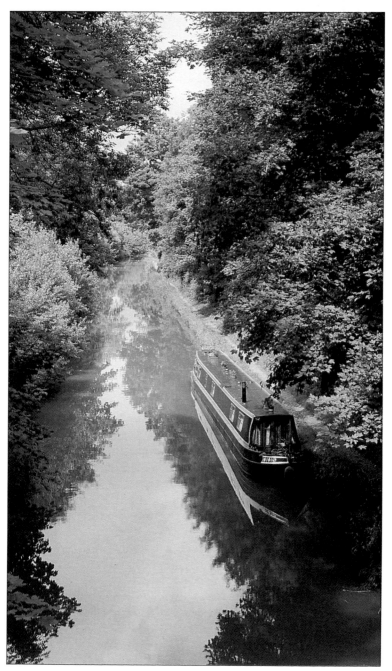

A narrow boat on the Grand Union Canal, which stretches from London to Derbyshire.

Emerging from the woods, the way is clearly signposted along the edge of the hill where the earthworks of Grim's Ditch become more obvious. Below, milky blue waters have flooded the scar of a pit where chalk was extracted to feed the cement works. The narrow chalk track is easy to distinguish along the lip of the hill. Here it is best to stay on the uphill side of Grim's Ditch and the path is now just a grassy route to the left of a fence with the final destination, Ivinghoe Beacon **76**, clearly visible on the immediate horizon. Also visible is Pitstone windmill, one of the oldest postmills in the country. Owned by the National Trust, it is open in the afternoon on summer Sundays and bank holidays. Do not be tempted to stray down the hill following the line of the ditch and bank; the occasional waymark makes the route evident. The pits on the hillside are thought to be the remains of prehistoric flint mines; flints have been found in the area.

The descent from Pitstone Hill to the minor road between Ivinghoe and Aldbury takes you well to the right of the hill, over a stile into the picnic area, then left onto the road and right through the kissing gate opposite the entrance to the car park. Now almost at the end of the journey, after all the ups and downs of the previous days, you remember that you are walking along a ridgeway. But there is one more valley to cross and one more ascent to make – the final one on to Ivinghoe Beacon itself.

The route ahead is obvious enough, on a track through arable crops. Follow it towards the triangle of trees ahead. Although Ivinghoe Beacon is not a particularly imposing hill, its isolation and position are good reasons why it should have been used as a beacon hill. Crossing the field on a hard, chalky white path you begin gently to ascend. Somehow the last few miles of any long-distance walk seem to be the longest and hardest. Perhaps this is the result of anticipating the end of one's efforts and relaxing a bit prematurely.

Having crossed the field, go through a gate and into sheep grazing land, then begin the ascent of Steps Hill, one of the Ivinghoe hills. Incombe Hole to the left is a deep curving gully carved into the hillside. Just as you reach the woodland, bear left and continue to rise steadily. Approaching the summit of Steps Hill, you can look back and see the path you have trodden. It looks a long way indeed and, although you cannot see it, you have journeyed 85 miles (137 km). This may be an easy drive of only a couple of hours by car but it seems much longer on foot.

At the summit of Steps Hill, the track forks to the right through a gate by a stile. This is a permissive bridleway maintained by the National Trust. The Ridgeway, however, goes to the left of the stile and strikes north-west across a field to the edge of scrub. The path through the hawthorn, although on well-drained chalk, can be muddy in winter since it is sheltered from the drying effect of the wind. As you emerge from the thicket, head down the hill and turn right through a gate in the fence. Follow the path and continue across open ground to the road.

Cross the road with care before the final, undulating climb up a broad track. After about 33 yards, turn left towards the Beacon. The final ascent is on a steep, chalky, rutted path which could be very slippery when it is wet. From the top of the Beacon, reached breathless but satisfied, there are superb views in all directions. As well as the trig point at 757 feet (230 metres) there is a stone cairn with a map on top, showing the route you

Contours are given in metres
The vertical interval is 5m

The chalk grassland slopes of Ivinghoe Beacon, which signify the end – or start – of the Ridgeway.

have walked and some landmarks on the way, to indicate that you have reached the end of your journey.

The walk is done and it is now just a matter of finding one's way home. The easiest way to the village of Ivinghoe is along the B489, which does have a pavement for walkers. Ivinghoe has a smart restaurant for anyone who wishes to celebrate their endeavours in style, and there is a youth hostel in the Old Brewery House with a pub a little further up the road towards Pitstone. You might like to visit the 13th century church of St Mary the Virgin, which has a thatch hook once used to pull burning thatch from houses to prevent fire from spreading and, beneath it, there is a man trap.

If you feel like walking further, Ivinghoe Beacon is not just the end (or beginning) of the Ridgeway; it is also the start of the Two Ridges Link to the Greensand Ridge Walk, and the Icknield Way if you fancy going on to Suffolk. But perhaps that is for another day, and another journey.

PART THREE

USEFUL
INFORMATION

Transport

The *Ridgeway Public Transport* leaflet (see page 141) provides details of public transport services to and from the Ridgeway. However, to help you plan your outings along the Ridgeway, a checklist of towns and villages served by public transport follows (listed from west to east). All destination towns listed have a train service except for those marked with an asterisk (*).

Avebury: buses to Marlborough*, Devizes*, Swindon and Salisbury

Ogbourne St George: buses to Swindon and Marlborough*

Wanborough: buses to Swindon, Marlborough* and Newbury

Bishopstone: buses to Swindon and Newbury

Ashbury: buses to Swindon and Newbury

Woolstone: buses to Swindon

Uffington: buses to Swindon

Childrey: buses to Wantage*

Letcombe Regis: buses to Wantage*

Wantage: buses to Oxford and Didcot as well as to local villages

Lockinge and Ardington: buses to Wantage*, Didcot and Oxford

West Ilsley: buses to Newbury (infrequent)

East Ilsley: buses to Oxford and Newbury (infrequent)

Compton: buses to Oxford and Newbury (infrequent)

Goring/Streatley: trains to Oxford, Reading and London and buses to Wallingford*, Reading and Oxford

North Stoke: buses to Wallingford* and Goring

Wallingford: buses to Oxford, Reading and London

Nuffield: buses to Wallingford*, Oxford and London

Watlington: buses to Oxford, Reading, High Wycombe and Aylesbury

Lewknor: buses to Watlington, Reading, High Wycombe and Aylesbury

Aston Rowant: buses to Oxford, High Wycombe and London

Chinnor: buses to High Wycombe and Thame

Princes Risborough: trains to London and Aylesbury and buses to Reading, Aylesbury, High Wycombe and Milton Keynes

Great Kimble: buses to Reading, High Wycombe and Aylesbury

Little Kimble: trains to London and buses to High Wycombe and Aylesbury

Wendover: trains to London and Aylesbury and buses to Aylesbury

Wigginton: buses to Chesham and Tring

Tring: trains to London and Milton Keynes and buses to Luton, Oxford, Aylesbury, Hemel Hempstead, Watford, Swindon, Bristol and Lowestoft.

Ivinghoe: buses to Luton and Aylesbury

Rail

National Rail, tel 0345 484 950 for information on services to all stations

From London

Paddington Station – Intercity to Swindon, Didcot, Reading, Newbury, Oxford, Pewsey. Local service to Goring-on-Thames.

Marylebone Station – local services to Saunderton, Princes Risborough, Little Kimble, Wendover.

Euston Station – local service to Tring.

St Pancras Station – local service to Luton.

From the West Country and South Wales

Intercity to Swindon, Didcot, Reading, Newbury, Pewsey.

From the Midlands and the North

Intercity to Oxford, Didcot, Reading, Luton.

From the South Coast

Intercity to Reading and Luton.

Accommodation and facilities

The *Ridgeway Information and Accommodation Guide* (see page 141) includes many addresses for accommodation, stabling, campsites and hostels together with details on other towns and village facilities. To help you plan your journey here is a check-list of local facilities (listed from west to east).

Key: po = post office   acc = accommodation
       ph = public house   st = stabling
       gs = general stores   c = camping
        t = telephone   yh = youth hostel
        r = restaurant/café
       wc = lavatories
        b = bank

Devizes: All town services, *acc*
Honeystreet: *ph, acc*
Pewsey: *po, ph, gs, t, wc, b, acc, st*
Marlborough: All town services, *acc*
Wootton Rivers: *ph, t, acc*
Lockeridge: *ph, acc, t, acc*
West Overton: *po, ph, gs, t, acc*
Avebury: *po, ph, gs, t, r, wc, acc*
Winterbourne Monkton: *po, ph, t, acc,*
Winterbourne Bassett: *ph, t*
Broad Hinton: *po, ph, t, gs*
Barbury Castle Country Park: *r, wc, acc, c*
Swindon: All town services; *acc*
Ogbourne St George: *ph, t, acc, st, c*
Aldbourne: *po, ph, gs, t, r, wc*
Wroughton: *po, ph, gs, wc*
Liddington: *po, ph, gs, t, acc*
Wanborough: *po, ph, t, acc, gs*
Bishopstone: *ph, t, acc*
Ashbury: *po, ph, gs, t, r, acc*
Woolstone: *ph, t, acc*
Uffington: *po, ph, gs, t, acc, st, c*
Kingston Lisle: *ph, t*
Westcot/Sparsholt: *ph, t, acc, st, c*
Childrey: *po, ph, gs, t, acc*
Letcombe Regis: *ph, t, acc, yh, st, c*
Wantage: All town services, *st, acc*
Ardington: *po, ph, gs, t, r, acc, st*
West Hendred: *ph, t*
East Hendred: *ph, po, t, acc, st*
Chilton: *po, ph, gs, t, r, acc*
Upton: *po, ph, t*
Blewbury: *po, ph, gs, t*
West Ilsley: *po, ph, gs*
East Ilsley: *po, ph, gs, t, acc*
Compton: *po, ph, gs, t, b, acc, st, c*
Aldworth: *po, ph, gs, t*
Streatley: *ph, t, yh*
Goring: *po, ph, gs, t, b, acc*
Moulsford: *ph, t, acc*
South Stoke: *ph, gs, c*
North Stoke: *ph, t, acc*

Wallingford: All town services, *acc*
Benson: *po, ph, gs, t, acc, st*
Nuffield: *ph, t, acc, c*
Swyncombe: *acc, st*
Nettlebed: *po, ph, gs, t*
Pishill: *ph, acc, st*
Watlington: All town services, *acc*
Chalgrove: *po, ph, gs, t, acc*
Lewknor: *po, ph, gs, t, acc*
Aston Rowant: *ph, t, acc*
Kingston Blount: *t, ph*
Chinnor: *po, ph, gs, t*
Bledlow: *ph, t*
Saunderton Lee: *ph, t*
Saunderton Station: *ph, t, acc*
Bradenham: *ph, t, yh*
Princes Risborough: All town services, *acc*
Whiteleaf: *ph*
Askett: *ph, t, acc, st*
Great & Little Kimble: *ph, t*
Butlers Cross: *ph, t*
Wendover: All town services, *acc*
The Lee: *po, ph, acc*
Wigginton: *po, ph, gs, t*
Tring: All town services
Tring Station: *ph, acc*
Berkhamsted: All town services
Aldbury: *po, ph, gs, t, r*
Pitstone: *gs, t, ph, r*
Ivinghoe: *po, ph, gs, t, yh, c, r*
Edlesborough: *po, ph, gs, t, acc*
Totternhoe: *po, ph, gs, t, acc*

Tourist information centres

Seasonal centres at:
Avebury: tel. (01672) 539425
Faringdon: The Pump House, 5 Market Place, Faringdon, Oxon
   SN7 7HL, tel. (01367) 242191

Centres open all year:

Swindon: 37 Regent Street, Swindon, Wilts SN1 1JL, tel. (01793) 530328/493007

Marlborough: Car park, George Lane, Marlborough, Wilts SN8 1EE, tel. (01672) 513989

Abingdon: 25 Bridge Street, Abingdon, Oxon OX14 3HN, tel. (01235) 522711

Wallingford: Town Hall, Market Place, Wallingford, Oxon OX10 0EG, tel. (01491) 826972

Reading: Town Hall, Blagrave Street, Reading, Berks RG1 1QH, tel. (0118) 9566226

High Wycombe: 6 Cornmarket, High Wycombe, Bucks HP11 2BW, tel. (01494) 421892

Thame: Market House, North Street, Thame, Oxon OX9 3HH, tel. (01844) 212834

Aylesbury: 8 Bourbon Street, Aylesbury, Bucks HP20 2RR, tel. (01296) 330559

Wendover: The Clock Tower, High Street, Wendover, Bucks HP22 6DU, tel. (01296) 696759

Dunstable: The Library, Vernon Place, Dunstable, Beds LU5 4HA, tel. (01582) 471012

Luton: Bus Station, Bute Street, Luton, Beds LU1 2EY, tel. (01582) 401579

Responsibility for the Ridgeway

The Ridgeway was designated a National Trail by the Countryside Commission in 1973. A National Trails Officer and other staff are funded by the Commission and employed by Oxfordshire County Council to manage the trail in conjunction with the five local councils – Wiltshire, Oxfordshire, West Berkshire, Buckinghamshire and Hertfordshire – through which the Ridgeway passes.

The Countryside Commission also funds the majority of the maintenance work. Much of the important practical work such as monitoring the route, litter collecting, signposting, vegetation clearance and habitat management is carried out by enthusiastic and committed members of the Ridgeway Volunteer Scheme under the guidance of Ridgeway staff.

The Ridgeway Office has developed a range of useful publications and merchandise. The following are sold (prices on request):

Information & Accommodation Guide: a regularly updated booklet full of essential information for people undertaking a long distance journey on the Ridgeway.

Ridgeway Information Pack: pack of leaflets. Seven leaflets cover the history and natural history of the National Trail, and information for walkers, horseriders, cyclists, vehicle users and volunteers.

Ridgeway Routes Pack: contains a series of circular walks from the Ridgeway and current programmes of events.

Let's Hear it for the Ridgeway!: a family activity book full of information and stimulating ideas of things to see and do, on and around the Ridgeway.

Badges, sweatshirts and T-shirts with sporting logo.

The following are available free on receipt of a large stamped addressed envelope:

Public Transport leaflet; Events Programme.

All queries and requests for information should be addressed to: Ridgeway Office, Countryside Service, Department of Leisure and Arts, Holton, Oxford OX33 1QQ, tel. Oxford (01865) 810224; fax (01865) 810207.
Email: mail@rway-tpath.demon.co.uk

A voluntary society, Friends of the Ridgeway, also takes an interest in the National Trail. New members are welcomed and enquiries should be directed to the address on page 143.

Regional recreational routes

A number of regional routes for walking and riding connect with the Ridgeway and therefore provide the opportunity for further extensive journeys on foot or on horseback. The addresses of the organizations mentioned below are given on pages 142–3.

The Wessex Ridgeway: a 137-mile (220-km) walk from Lyme Regis in Dorset to Marlborough. Devised by the Ramblers' Association and obtainable from their London office.

The Thames Path: The National Trail from the source of the river in Gloucestershire to the Thames Barrier in London, a distance of 180 miles (288 km). The official National Trail guidebook is *The Thames Path* by David Sharp, published by Aurum Press. Further information on the Thames Path can be obtained from the National Trails Office above.

Swan's Way: a 65-mile (104-km) long-distance bridleway which runs from Goring-on-Thames to Salcey Forest in Northants. This coincides with the Ridgeway for much of its length and provides a route for cyclists and horse riders as far as Bledlow. For details contact Buckinghamshire County Council.

The Icknield Way Riders' Route: a 23-mile (37 km) route for walkers, cyclists and horseriders from Bledlow to Pitstone, near the end of the Ridgeway at Ivinghoe Beacon. It runs parallel to, or shares, the Ridgeway for much of the route.

The d'Arcy Dalton Way: a 65-mile (104-km) walking route across west Oxfordshire, linking the Ridgeway at Wayland's Smithy with the Thames Path, Oxfordshire Way and Oxford Canal towpath at Wormleighton Reservoir in Warwickshire. Details from Oxford Fieldpaths Society.

Oxfordshire Way: a 67-mile (104-km) walking route from Henley-on-Thames to Bourton-on-the-Water in Gloucestershire. Links with the Ridgeway near Watlington. Details from Oxfordshire County Council.

Icknield Way: a 100-mile (160-km) walking route between Ivinghoe Beacon and Thetford, the start of Peddars Way. A bridle route from Princes Risborough to Thetford is due to open shortly. Details from Icknield Way Association.

North Bucks Way: a 35-mile (48-km) cross-country walk from the Ridgeway near Chequers to Wolverton near Milton Keynes. Details from Buckinghamshire County Council.

South Bucks Way: a connecting 23-mile (37-km) walk between the Ridgeway at Coombe Hill and the Grand Union Canal at Denham. Details from Buckinghamshire County Council.

Two Ridges Link: an 8-mile (13-km) connection between the Ridgeway at Ivinghoe Beacon and the Greensand Ridge walk at Leighton Buzzard. Details from Buckinghamshire County Council.

Lambourn Valley Way: a 22-mile (35-km) walk from Newbury to Uffington Castle. Details from West Berkshire Council.

Greensand Ridge Walk: a 30-mile (48-km) walk from Leighton Buzzard to Tetworth in Cambridge. Linked to the Ridgeway by the Two Ridges Link. Details from Bedfordshire County Council.

Other useful addresses

All Wheel Drive Club, PO Box 6, Fleet, Hampshire GU13 9YY
Backpackers Club, 49 Lyndhurst Road, Exmouth, Devon EX8
    3DS, tel. (01395) 265159

BBONT The Local Wildlife Trust, 3 Church Cowley Road, Cowley, Oxford OX4 3JR, tel. (01865) 775476

British Horse Society, British Equestrian Centre, Stoneleigh, Kenilworth, Warwickshire CV8 2LR, tel. (01203) 696697

Buckinghamshire County Council, Environmental Services Department, County Hall, Walton Street, Aylesbury HP21 7QQ, tel. (01296) 395000.

Byways & Bridleways Trust, PO Box 117, Newcastle upon Tyne NE3 5YT, tel. (0191) 2364086

Chiltern Society, PO Box 1029, Marlow, Bucks SL7 2HZ.

Council for the Protection of Rural England (CPRE), Warwick House, 25 Buckingham Palace Road, London SW1W 0PP, tel. 0171-976 6433

Countryside Commission (Headquarters), John Dower House, Crescent Place, Cheltenham, GL50 3RA, tel. (01242) 521 381

Countryside Commission (South East Regional Office), 4th Floor, 71 Kingsway, London WC2B 6ST, tel. 0171-831 3510

Cyclists' Touring Club Offroad, Cotterell House, 69 Meadrow, Godalming, Surrey GU7 3HS, tel. (01483) 417217

Endurance Horse and Pony Society of Great Britain, Mill House, Mill Lane, Stoke Bruerne, Northants NN12 7SH

Hertfordshire County Council, County Hall, Hertford SG13 8DN, tel. (01992) 555265

Friends of the Ridgeway, Mr Peter Gould, 18 Hampton Park, Bristol BS6 6LH

Icknield Way Association, Mr K. Payne, 19 The Ridgeway, Hitchin, Herts SG5 2BT, tel. (01462) 450089

Long Distance Walkers' Association, 10 Temple Park Close, Leeds, West Yorks LS15 0JJ, tel. (0113) 2642205

Motoring Organisations' Land Access & Recreation Association, PO Box 20, Market Drayton TF9 1WR, tel. (01630) 657627

National Trails Office, Countryside Service, Department of Leisure & Arts, Holton, Oxford OX33 1QQ, tel. (01865) 810224. Email: mail@rway-tpath.demon.co.uk

Ordnance Survey, Romsey Road, Maybush, Southampton SO9 4DH, tel. (01703) 792000

Oxfordshire County Council, Countryside Service, Dept of Leisure & Arts, Holton, Oxford OX33 1QQ, tel. (01865) 810226

Ramblers' Association, 1–5 Wandsworth Road, London SW8 2XX, tel. 0171-582 6878

Trail Riders Fellowship, PO Box 196, Derby DE1 9EY

Wiltshire Bridleways Association, 34 Langstone Way, Westlea, Swindon SN5 7BU, tel. (01793) 870885

Wiltshire County Council, Dept of Environmental Service, County Hall, Trowbridge, Wilts BA14 8JD, tel. (01225) 713000

Wiltshire Wildlife Trust, 18–19 High Street, Devizes, Wilts SN10 1AT, tel. (01380) 725670

Youth Hostels Association, Trevelyan House, 8 St Stephen's Hill, St Albans, Herts, AL1 2DY, tel. (01727) 855215

Bibliography

Bulfield, Anthony, *The Icknield Way* (Terence Dalton, 1972).

Bull, Andy and Barrett, Frank, *The Mountain Biker's Guide to the Ridgeway* (Stanley Paul, 1991).

Burden, Vera *et al, Discovering the Ridgeway* (Shire Publications, 1995).

Charles, Alan, *Exploring the Ridgeway* (Countryside Books, 1994).

Fitter, R. (eds.), *The Wildlife of the Thames Counties* (BBONT/ Robert Dugdale, 1985).

Godwin, Fay and Anderson, J.R.L., *The Oldest Road: An Exploration of the Ridgeway* (Whittet Books, 1992).

Ingrams, Richard, *The Ridgeway* (Phaidon Press, 1988).

Ordnance Survey Historical Guides, *Oxfordshire and Berkshire* (OS and George Philip, 1988).

Pitts, Michael, *Footprints through Avebury* (Stones Print, 1985).

Thomas, Edward, *The Icknield Way* (Wildwood, 1980).

de M. Vatcher, Faith and Vatcher, Lance, *The Avebury Monuments* (English Heritage, 1987).

Whynne-Hammond, Charles, *Pub Walks along the Ridgeway* (Countryside Books, 1997).

Ordnance Survey Maps covering the Ridgeway

Landranger Maps: 165, 173, 174, 175.

Explorer Maps: 3 Chiltern Hills South (to be re-published as Chiltern Hills West in spring 1999).

157 Marlborough and Savernake Forest.

170 Abingdon, Wantage and Vale of White Horse.

181 Chiltern Hills North.

Motoring Maps: Reach the Ridgeway area using Travelmaster 9, South East England.